THE
100% HORSE

How to create the go-anywhere, do-anything horse

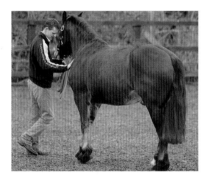

Michael Peace
and Lesley Bayley

D&C
David and Charles

All photography by BOB ATKINS
except Horsepix: pp 31, 33 and 129

A DAVID & CHARLES BOOK
David & Charles is a subsidiary of F+W (UK) Ltd.,
an F+W Publications Inc. company

First published in the UK in 2005

Distributed in North America
by F&W Publications, Inc.
4700 East Galbraith Road
Cincinnati, OH 45236
1-800-289-0963

A catalogue record for this book is available from
the British Library.

ISBN 0 7153 2099 8

Printed in China by SNP Leefung
for David & Charles
Brunel House   Newton Abbot   Devon

Commissioning Editor: Jane Trollope
Art Editor: Sue Cleave
Desk Editor: Louise Crathorne
Project Editor: Jo Weeks
Production: Beverley Richardson

Visit our website at www.davidandcharles.co.uk

David & Charles books are available from all
good bookshops; alternatively you can contact
our Orderline on (0)1626 334555 or write to us at
FREEPOST EX2110, David & Charles Direct, Newton
Abbot, TQ12 4ZZ (no stamp required UK mainland).

Contents

Introduction

Believing that something is possible is the first step to creating your 100% horse. It's easy to make excuses and avoid the challenges ahead, not just with our horses but in the rest of our lives too. We can convince ourselves that it's only exceptional people who achieve great results when, in fact, the only difference is that pioneers and great achievers, like Sir Roger Bannister who ran the first four minute mile or Sir Edmund Hillary who climbed Mount Everest, are not limited in their beliefs. Seeing something *is* possible changes our belief systems and raises the bar in terms of what we accept we *can* and *can't* achieve.

With the correct approach and encouragement, horses – and people for that matter – are capable of exceptional things, and in many cases, the biggest ingredients lacking are inspiration and the confidence to go for the next level. Each day in my work with horses and their owners I demonstrate that with the right approach and tools both horses and people are capable of achieving things they hadn't dared to dream of before and this was the inspiration for this book.

Taking on a horse is a big commitment in terms of time and money, and many owners have a huge emotional investment in their horse as well. So it is not easy to be objective when working out why your horse won't canter on the left rein/jump drop fences/hack out sensibly, and so on. Could it be you? Does the horse have a physical limitation? Is it a training problem?

This book will help you solve niggling problems and improve your relationship with your horse. It will set you on the way to having a horse that will do anything and go anywhere. Whatever your current experience, as you put into practice the ideas and exercises you will learn a great deal about your horse, and horses in general:

- how they think and behave
- how they show that they are in pain or discomfort
- how to understand their personalities
- how to recognize whether they are experiencing a genuine problem or simply being unco-operative
- how to persuade them to co-operate
- how to construct a progressive training programme that is suited to your horse's needs

It is especially important to have a well-behaved horse if you keep him in a busy yard, but you can also use this sort of environment to your advantage by enabling your horse to experience some of the wide variety of events that occur every day within such a yard.

You will also learn how vital it is to control your own emotions so that you can best help your horse. Through all this, you'll gain a much greater understanding of how your horse's body and mind work, and how you need to consider these as you ride and train your horse.

When you are working on improving your horse, the important point to remember is to do something positive every day to build towards your ultimate goal of having a 100% horse. You will have to devote time to your horse – nothing is achieved without some effort – but if you invest time wisely now, you will save time in years to come. An example: one of the commonest problems is a horse that will not load. When you first have your horse, if you invest *whatever time is necessary* in showing him that loading is not a fearful experience, then you will save many hours of frustration later. Once a horse realizes that he is not going to endanger himself and makes a conscious decision to load into a trailer, he will continue to do it. (Obviously, if the horse is involved in an accident in a trailer, or has a bad journey, then

he will have to be re-schooled to load again.) And this doesn't only apply to loading.

Horses are generally very passive and co-operative animals, as in their natural state they live in herds where every member works for the common good and survival. Domesticated horses have much to deal with in our world – being transported in trailers, living in stables, having shoes put on their feet, being saddled and having someone sit on their back. Even though we might regard these events as part of everyday life, for a horse they are very much against his natural instincts. In fact, all these activities are completely alien to him – it's a tribute to the horses' generosity of spirit that they allow us to train them to accept domesticated life. It is our responsibility to show our appreciation and carry out any training that is required with sensitivity and awareness of a horse's needs. If he is frightened we need to give him time, to reassure him and prove to him that he *can* do what we are asking.

Punishing a frightened horse is pointless and merely

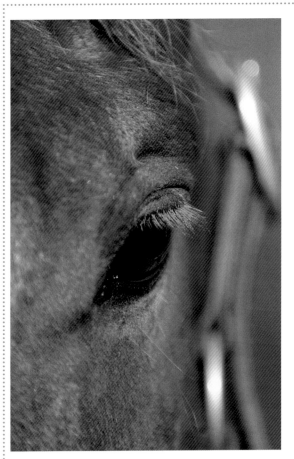

how to achieve success

- Don't dwell on the history, it's the future that counts.
- Keep an open mind.
- Learn to listen to your horse.
- Apply the techniques in a structured, logical way so that you build a solid foundation of training.
- Take your time – don't rush or miss things out.
- Don't make assumptions – just because your horse has always bucked as he goes into canter, doesn't mean that he has to be like that, or he enjoys being like that. There could well be a physical reason for his behaviour. Equally, don't assume that because he could do something well yesterday that he will perform just as well today. Horses (and humans!) have off days.
- Remember there is a reason for everything the horse does.
- Think about your horse holistically. Many different factors affect him, for example, how he is shod, fed, or ridden, whether his saddle fits, whether he is in the correct environment, and so on.
- Treat your horse with the respect you would like to receive yourself – a horse is a living, sentient being and he deserves nothing less.

highlights the trainer's inadequacies. To avoid being in this situation, you need to learn to recognize and understand the many signs that your horse uses to tell you how he is feeling. Some of these signs may be very clear – planting himself at the bottom of the trailer ramp – others can be much more subtle – a slight flinch as the saddle is placed upon his back. Usually a horse politely lets you know that there is a problem. However, if his signs go unnoticed, he will have to be more insistent in his communications. Take the true example of a horse who had a badly fitting saddle. At first he started to move away when the rider appeared with the saddle, then he started snapping at her as she tried to place the saddle on his back, ultimately, he refused to have the saddle anywhere near him, plunging and bucking to avoid it. This is when the rider asked for help. Now she knows what was happening, and in future she will recognize a problem much sooner. Learning to spot problems early on, and to deal with them, means that you save yourself and your horse a great deal of grief.

A horse has a reason for everything he does. Unfortunately, some horse people do not comprehend this very simple point, and as a result some horses have had very unpleasant experiences, perhaps being badly treated or worked when they were in pain. Such horses can become aggressive and difficult to handle or may become switched off and depressed. Either way, it's not a pleasant situation for horse or rider.

It is possible to help these horses and re-train them but it takes much time and an experienced, sensitive trainer. The better scenario is to avoid getting into such a bad situation in the first place – and this book will help. Use it to guide you through physical points to be aware of and to learn about how to deal with various situations. It will enable you to build solid foundations in your horse's training, so that he can accept whatever life throws at him. You can use the exercises for a young horse who knows nothing or to re-train an older horse that is somewhat sceptical about life. The approach is always the same (see 10 steps to a 100% horse).

10 steps to a 100% horse

1 Understand your horse's personality.
2 Understand yourself. Consider how your personality affects how you handle your horse. Do you suit each other or are you likely to clash? If the latter, remember that it is easier for you to change your attitude and control your feelings, than it is for the horse to do so.
3 Eliminate any physical problems for your horse.
4 Allow yourself the time you need to get the job done.
5 Set everything up for success. You want to help your horse to succeed, so ensure you have control over all the factors that you can influence.
6 Be clear about your goal but be flexible enough to deal with whatever the horse can offer on that day.
7 Keep control of your emotions. Never let temper get the better of you!
8 Work with your horse through the exercise, watching him second by second, rewarding him for his efforts.
9 Be particular, firm, fair and consistent in your handling of your horse.
10 Finish each session on a good note and show your horse you are pleased with his efforts.

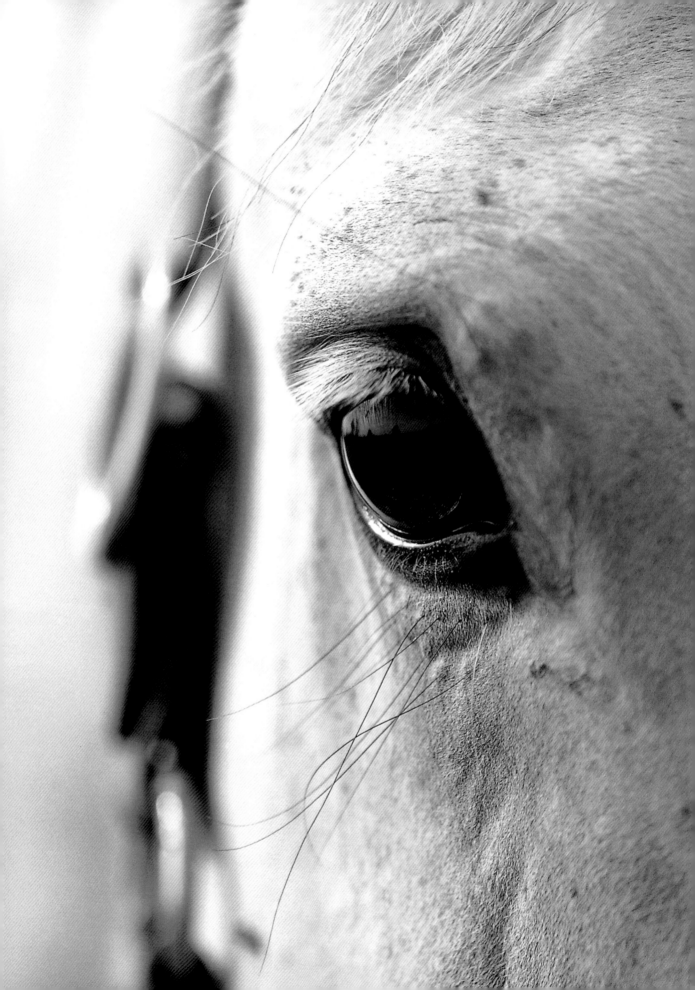

1 Listen to Your Horse

Your horse is rather like a painting. The genuine, unspoilt young horse is like a blank canvas: he has no hang-ups or problems and you have the opportunity to create a masterpiece. Through careful and progressive training you can produce a horse that does what he is asked, willingly and to the best of his ability. However, if you get the training wrong, you could create a horse that is extremely confused and anxious – your canvas will resemble something that looks like an explosion in a paint factory!

Older horses are like a frequently altered or unfinished painting. They may have started out as enthusiastic, well-trained youngsters, but experience of people has added extra layers of paint to the canvas. Some of these layers may be okay, others may represent dreadful experiences. In order to get at the real genuine horse underneath, the trainer has to strip away all the rubbish. In addition he has to rejuvenate the original canvas, so exposing the horse's true nature. This can take time – the horse may have been protecting himself physically (because of pain), emotionally (because of bad experiences with people, or factors such as a bad weaning, being separated from a very close friend, either equine or human) and mentally (because he has been overfaced, overtrained, misunderstood). The horse may well be carrying lots of 'baggage' with him – this section will give you an idea of how to recognize some of this baggage.

Know your horse

If you want to produce a horse that is 100% you must first learn to really observe your horse. To be a successful trainer you must be aware of your horse's reactions at all times, to be a successful horsemaster you need to recognize immediately when something is amiss – so the first thing to learn is to look at your horse and to see. This might sound obvious but many owners cannot answer simple questions such as 'Can your horse stand square?' or 'Does he always drag his offhind toe?'. You need to know what your horse's usual reactions are, otherwise how do you know when something is wrong?

1 The horse's eyes are the windows to his soul. This horse is a gentle character, which is reflected in his eyes. Look at the horses you know. Can you distinguish the worriers from the laid-back, happy characters? Have you spotted the horse where 'the lights are on, but no-one's at home'? Occasionally you'll meet the aggressive horse – or an angry horse. His feelings will be shown in his eyes – and the only way you can learn about this is to look and see.

2 & 3 How does your horse interact with you and with other horses? What is his approach to life? To work with him successfully, you need to understand his life and the issues affecting it. This horse comes to call for his owner, co-author Lesley, and is happy to stay with her, even when she turns him loose. His introduction to people, including vets, farriers and dentists, was pleasant and thoughtful, which means he happily stands for shoeing and so on. He has learned that these everyday things are not to be feared.

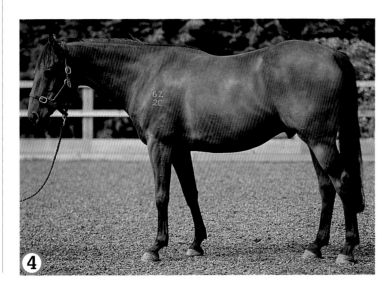

4 Your horse's upbringing and personality affect how he works – and so does his conformation. Be realistic in assessing him, both statically, as here, and dynamically (5 and 6). It is only by recognizing his shortcomings that you can learn how to cope with them. This horse is three-quarters Thoroughbred and a quarter Irish Draught. He had undergone very little schooling when this photograph was taken. Overall he has good conformation and is well-proportioned, but he does have a short back. This has meant he had to have a tailor-made saddle, which is worth the expense as it will avoid back problems.

what to look for when your horse is moving

- Look at the joints. Does he flex them evenly. For example, is he using his hocks evenly or is one working harder. If one hock is working harder look at the other joints in the hindleg – stifle, hip, fetlock. Are these doing more or less work? How does the picture differ from offside to nearside? Does a change of rein make any difference?

- Check whether he is tracking up. Consider how his conformation might affect his ability to track up. Long-backed horses will find it more difficult. Does he have the stride length you'd expect, bearing in mind his breeding and size? If you lunge him with his saddle on, does his stride become more restricted?

- How does his back look? Can you see the muscles working over the lumbar area? If he looks stiff or tight through this area, he will have problems in stretching along his topline.

- What is he doing with his head? If he is tilting it, there could be several reasons for this including a misalignment in the atlas (the first bone in the neck), muscle soreness, dental problems or having a rider who is stronger in that hand, which means the horse is used to going in that way.

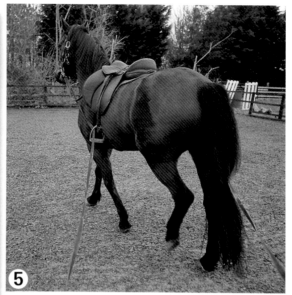

5 Long reining gives you the opportunity to see how your horse moves from behind. Does he uses each half of his hindquarters evenly or is one side working harder? Is he moving straight? Does he have a tendency to swing one hindleg in an outwards arc, or does he bring one hindleg across his midline?

6 Lungeing your horse gives you the chance to see him move on both reins. Keep the lunge rein loose as you want him to move in his own balance, rather than leaning on a tight lunge rein. Note what he offers of his own accord. This horse is being quite lazy, he is barely tracking up and his back is a little stiff.

Static physical check-up

If you suspect your horse has physical problems, then he probably has. The various static checks you can try are shown here and on pages 14–15. Get to know your horse's body. Use your hands to feel the skin and muscles, noting if he flinches when touched anywhere, such as over the back muscles, at the base of the neck, where the girth goes, in the lumbar area or along his hindquarter muscles. Use only light pressure as any horse will react if he is prodded. Lightly run your fingers either side of the horse's spine so that you can feel any peculiar lumps or bumps. Take note of what you find and ask a therapist (see box) to explain your findings.

1 Either side of the withers is a common area for a horse to have muscle wastage. Often a badly fitting saddle is the cause, although tight, badly fitting rugs can also affect this area. Horses may also have muscular problems, perhaps because of skeletal misalignments and consequent inadequate nerve function, which leads to the muscle atrophying.

2 Therapists use their hands to check for soreness in the muscles or misalignments of the skeletal structure. Here the neck is being checked. If the area is sore the horse will throw up his head, move away suddenly or his muscles may go into spasm.

choosing a therapist

Get help from a reputable therapist, such as a McTimoney chiropractor to make skeletal adjustments, an Equine Muscle Release Therapist to work directly on the muscles but affecting the horse's entire body, or a physiotherapist. If your horse has dental problems, consult an equine dental technician (have your horse's teeth checked at least once a year, preferably twice). Most therapists will explain what they are doing and why, and will help you recognize the signs that your horse gives when all is not well.

3 There are various means of palpating a horse. Just feeling with the hands, exerting minimal pressure, can elicit startling responses if a horse is sore in a particular area. However, some horses deal with a problem by blocking out the pain, which means that there may not be any response at all, even though the therapist is touching what would normally be a reflex point. This horse shows no evidence of a badly fitted saddle and so palpation in the withers does not produce any flinching. If a horse has evidence of trauma in this area, such as muscle atrophy or white hairs, then palpation often shows that he is sore.

4 Palpation on normal reflex points involves a light squeeze and release motion. If horses are sore in the lumbar area they will quickly sink away as this area is palpated. The reaction can be extreme – in very bad cases the horse almost sits down – or nothing may happen, but this is not a good sign, either.

5 A light squeeze on the hindquarter muscles either side of the tail can indicate a great deal about the state of the hindquarter muscles. It is like grabbing hold of the inside of your leg, at the top. It should not hurt at all. However, when you do this simple move on some horses, they tuck their hindquarters under and the muscles go tight and hard.

6 This horse is sore in his hindquarter muscles and has reacted to the simple tail test (see 5), by tucking under his pelvis and tightening his muscles – compare this to photograph 5. You can see how the muscles have tightened and how the two halves of his hindquarters are emphasized separately.

7 Look at this horse's reaction when he is touched at the base of the neck. His neck muscles are tense; indeed the rest of his body is also showing excessive tension. There has to be a reason for this tension – the most common cause is discomfort or pain.

8 There is relatively poor muscle development either side of the horse's spine and his hindquarters are under-developed.

9 The horse is also rather tight over the lumbar area – if you think of the horse as a car, then the energy and propulsion being generated by the hindquarters is not being transmitted particularly well to the driveshaft (horse's trunk) and steering (horse's front end). Take the chance to feel your horse and any other horse you can examine, so that you can recognize when a horse shows excessive tension in his lumbar area.

be careful

Take care when running your hands over your horse – some horses are so sore that they can barely tolerate being touched. Even horses that are normally gentle and easy going can exhibit extreme and unexpected reactions if touched in a sore spot. Horses may suddenly kick out, bite, buck or rear. Remember that horses reacting out of pain should not be punished – this would be an added injustice.

other signs of discomfort

Take a holistic view of your horse and consider behaviour that may well have its roots in pain. For example, horses that dislike being girthed up are often sore in certain pectoral muscles, horses that clamp their tails when tail bandages are applied are often sore in their hindquarter muscles, horses that scrape up their bedding into a pile and then stand in it, often do so to ease lower back pain.

10 Horses, like people, are not completely symmetrical. Get to know your horse, so you can understand where a lack of symmetry is having effects. With the horse's neck straight, check the gap between the bottom of the atlas and the jawbone (mandible). A marked difference either side indicates the atlas is out of alignment. A McTimoney chiropractor can rectify this. Look at the horse's head from in front and the side, noting differences such as between the levels of the eyes and nostrils. A severe head tilt due to an atlas problem has been known to make one eye look bigger than the other.

If your horse persistently carries his head in the air he will be sore in the neck, sore in the girth area and in his back, because he will have constantly been moving with a hollowed back. As a result some muscles will be over-developed and others will be under-developed. This is not an efficient way of moving for the horse and the weakening of his back muscles makes it even more difficult for him to carry the rider. This situation is setting the horse up for discomfort and ultimately resistances.

If your horse has a break in his muscular development, such as a dip in the neck, it is often because he has been worked incorrectly, often in a 'gadget'. While there may be a place for some training aids, in certain circumstances, it is all too easy to create more problems than you are trying to solve. If you do want to use a gadget or training aid make sure you know precisely what you are trying to achieve, how to use it effectively and what not to do with it.

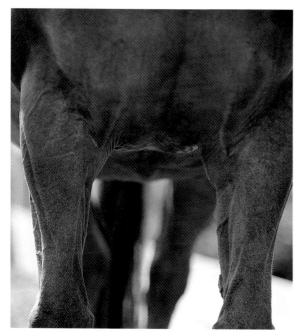

When you look at a horse side on and from in front, you should be able to see well-defined muscles. This horse has a very poorly developed thoracic sling (the strap of muscles that attach the front legs to the horse's body). This is because his pectorals are exceedingly tense, which is caused by skeletal problems and inadequate nerve function.

eliminate the obvious

If you are experiencing problems with your horse eliminate obvious sources of pain or problems. Here is a checklist of sources of problems and how to tackle them:

- Teeth – Get teeth checked by an equine dental technician. Unless a gag is used, it is difficult for anyone to find out what is happening right at the back of a horse's mouth.

- Muscles and bones – Find out, by word of mouth recommendation, about good chiropractors, muscle therapists and physiotherapists who can assist you.

- Diet – Is your horse's diet correct? Feed manufacturers offer helplines with access to advice from qualified nutritionists. Take advantage of these.

- Tack – Have your saddle checked. Horses change shape quickly and even a bespoke saddle may, within a matter of weeks, no longer fit your horse.

- Rugs – If rugs pull back on the withers they can create problems. Don't try to save money by not replacing ill-fitting rugs.

Dynamic physical check-up

There are several ways in which to develop your eye for how a horse is moving. Get together with friends and observe how all your horses move, from in front, behind and from the side. Watch them when they are walked on grass, a hard surface and in an arena, as certain problems may show up more on different surfaces. For further practice, go along to veterinary inspections at events such as horse trials or endurance rides, and watch horses in racecourse parade rings or as they are being ridden in showing classes.

the run up

- Ask someone to lead the horse towards and away from you in a straight line, so that you can assess him from directly in front and behind.
- At the end of the school ask your helper to turn the horse away from him. On the next walk down, ask the helper to turn the horse towards him. This allows you to see each hindleg turning.
- Ask the helper to walk him past you from side-to-side so that you can check the horse's action on both sides, too.

1 As the horse walks towards you check how he moves his front legs. Is the movement of one slightly more restricted, or are they both used equally? Does he turn his feet out or brush the hooves together? Watch the horse from the side and check whether he tracks up. Is there any difference in the way he uses each fore or hindleg?

2 As he walks away, look at the horse's tail – it should swing easily from side to side. Horses that hold their tail out to one side or clamp it down normally have tense hindquarter muscles. (Bear in mind the horse's breed; Arabs, for example, will often carry their tails out behind.) As the turn is made at the end of the school, note whether the horse is stepping under himself quite easily. Look out for shuffling around a turn, with the horse taking small steps instead of easy smooth flowing ones.

3 Observe each half of the hindquarters and how they relate to each other. The ideal is to see an equal swinging motion with even use of the joints and a relaxed tail. Some horses have a predominant swing to one side, some horses look really stiff in both. Look at the croup (highest point on the hindquarters). This is formed by the two sides of the top of the horse's pelvis (the tuber sacrale) and both sides should be level. If a horse is thought to be lame behind, a vet will watch this point to decide which leg has the problem.

1 This horse shows how much of a difference there can be in the way the joints are moved. Here, the nearside hindleg is being lifted to take a stride and there is a reasonable degree of flexion in the stifle, hock and fetlock.

2 Here, the offside hindleg is being moved and it is clear that there is less flexion of the joints and the horse doesn't lift the leg as high to make the stride.

3 The hindlegs are also moved one across in front of the other, which could be due to excess tension in the adductor muscles, which move the horse's leg towards his body. Watch the front leg movement, too. Conformation will obviously play a part and boots can minimize risk of injury, if your horse brushes, for example.

muscle development tells a story

This horse has fairly even muscle development in the hindquarters – any asymmetry would indicate a problem. Carry out regular checks on your horse so that you can spot any changes early on. Check your horse on a level concrete surface and ensure he is standing square.

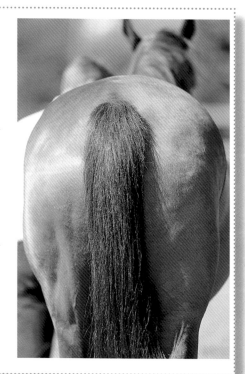

- Check hindquarter muscle development from behind. Look from the top of the croup and compare each side. The ideal is to have more or less perfect symmetry, some horses slope away more quickly on one side than the other.

- Check shoulders and withers from behind, looking downwards onto them. (You will probably need to stand on a box to do this, so don't risk it if it will upset your horse). Again, the ideal is for both sides to look equal. Most horses are not – one shoulder will look bigger – perhaps because the other shoulder has wasted muscle in comparison. If you can see dips either side of the withers this is muscle atrophy.

- Using a flexicurve, take a template of your horse's withers on a regular basis so you notice any changes.

Assessing yourself

How you ride and train your horse has an important impact upon his physical development and overall longevity. Invest in lessons from a reputable instructor and ensure that you follow a logical, progressive schooling programme. It is also important that you are checked regularly by a chiropractor. If you are not in balance, your horse will start to compensate for you, producing problems for himself.

Many riders have problems such as a misaligned pelvis and this can drastically affect their horse's way of going. Just as with the horses, if you address a skeletal problem, you should also consult a therapist specializing in muscles, as muscles move bones. For example, if your pelvis has been misaligned, the muscles will be used to holding it in the wrong position. A chiropractor can adjust the bones, but the muscles also need to be worked on too, otherwise they may pull the pelvis out again.

The balanced horse is the product of a balanced rider. Your physical imperfections have a profound effect on how your horse must adjust himself to carry you.

your horse will let you know

There are several ways in which your horse lets you know that you are not 100% physically. For example, you may find that it is difficult to ride him in a straight line. You may find rising trot on one diagonal feels more forced. You may even feel that you are twisted. Perhaps your horse always leans on one rein: this is often because you are heavier in that hand. If you notice that your horse is not going as well as normal and you know that he is fine, skeletally and muscularly, then you should get yourself checked.

If you haven't learned how to work a horse in-hand, take the opportunity to learn this technique. It's a great way to teach a horse a new skill before trying to do it from the saddle. It is also a way of observing how the horse moves, how he tackles new skills, whether he finds some movements more difficult than others, which rein he prefers and so on. If you are short of time or unable to ride, working in-hand offers an alternative option for exercise.

choosing and using therapists

If you decide that you would like a therapist to see your horse, you should first get permission from your vet. Any good therapist will ask you to do this – it's a legal requirement. Before a therapist does anything to your horse, he or she will take details of the horse's history and assess him. Reputable therapists will not mind being questioned about their training or being asked to explain what they are doing. Word of mouth is usually the best way to find a therapist. However, if someone is recommended to you but you do not feel at ease with how they relate to you or your horse, then find someone else.

Checking the saddle fits

Saddle fitting is a hot topic, with many people having strong feelings about certain types of saddle and even whether saddles do cause problems. However, therapists see the results of poorly fitting saddles on a regular basis. Access to good saddle fitters can be difficult and they do have a demanding job: the horse's conformation may make a good fit difficult to achieve, the owner may only want to spend a limited amount, the rider may not position the saddle in the correct place on the horse, the saddle may be used on more than one horse, and so on. However, there are some basic fitting rules that everyone should be aware of.

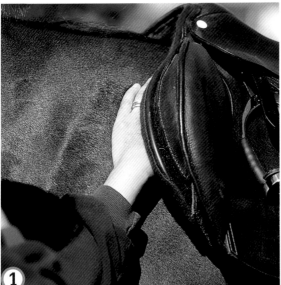

1 This saddle is too far forward and will interfere with the action of the horse's shoulder. Many people – including some professional riders – put the saddles too far forward.

2 The saddle is in the correct place, allowing the horse free movement of the shoulder. You should be able to feel your horse's scapula (shoulder blade), which extends from the withers to the shoulder joint. Place your arm along it, as shown, to check whether your normal placement of the saddle would cause interference with the shoulder.

3 Saddles must be clear of the spine all the way along the gullet. This clearance should be checked from front and back, with and without a rider in the saddle. The flocked panels should make contact with the horse's back along either side of the spine – if the saddle touches only at the front and back, it is 'bridging', which is not acceptable because it means the rider's weight is concentrated on four points instead of being spread along the entire bearing surface of the saddle.

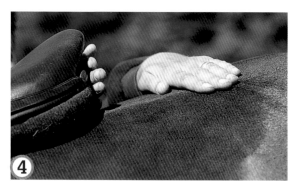

4 It is important that the saddle is the correct length for the horse. There should be a good hand's width from behind the saddle to the loins, so ensuring this vital area is not bearing any weight. A tall or large rider with a short-backed horse may have to have a shorter saddle than they would normally because of this. It is important that the horse's comfort and welfare is not compromised. The saddle should sit on the horse's back evenly so that the weight is distributed over the largest possible bearing surface. If the panels of the saddle curve upwards then the weight is again concentrated on to two points instead of being evenly distributed.

5 Place the saddle slightly too far forward, on the withers, then slide it back into position, taking into account the shoulders. Girth up and then check that it is in the correct position by seeing many fingers you can get in between the horse's elbow and the beginning of the girth. Here, it's only possible to fit two fingers, which means the saddle is too far forward.

6 This shows a hand's width between elbow and girth, which is a good rule of thumb for correct saddle position. Check this before and after exercise as some horses' conformation results in the saddle creeping forward.

holistic approach

When dealing with horses no single aspect should be taken in isolation. Even a horse with good conformation could be experiencing various problems. For instance, if his posture is poor, despite his good conformation, then pain is likely to be involved somewhere. This could be due to muscular problems, which in turn may be caused by compensation, perhaps because of an injury or accident or even something like poor shoeing. These photographs show a well-shod and well-balanced hoof. Take a good look at your horse's feet. The front feet should be a pair, as should the back feet. The hoof-pastern angle should be about 45 degrees in the front feet and 50 degrees in the back feet. If you find that your horse has one foot larger than the other this could be because of uneven weight distribution causing one foot to spread as it is taking more weight, while the other foot shrinks.

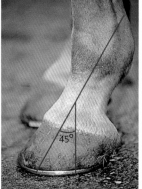

To overcome physical problems with your horse, you may well find yourself working with a combination of any of these people: vet; farrier; trainer; nutritionist; chiropractor; muscle therapist; dental technician and saddle fitter.

Assessing your horse's type

When I begin to train a horse it's important for me to have a good understanding of what I'm dealing with, so I make an assessment of a horse's character. This means I know exactly where to start and how to work with him. First impressions count for a lot, and if I'm too easy with a tough horse or too tough on a sensitive horse, I'll create negativity that will get in the way and we won't progress as smoothly as we could.

It's important to point out that this initial assessment is more intuitive than academic and is simply a starting point. I have to be completely open and ready to adjust my view of a horse as the training progresses. For example, at first glance, a horse may appear tough but as I begin to work sympathetically with him, he starts to change. Likewise, it may be that a horse that appears nervous on the surface is quite manipulating underneath.

Anyone who wants to work with horses has to be flexible in their thinking and take care not to hold on to any rigid assumptions. This allows you to adapt your training as the horse you are working with begins to learn. All horses have a soft side – even the most hardened cases – and the objective of training has got to be to nurture this soft side when it appears. To me it is vital that a horse doesn't feel 'labelled' and that he realizes, through my work, that he is being given the

Think Equus and the 50:50 relationship

While many horse riders, trainers and owners like to try to achieve a 51:49 relationship with their horse, I believe it should be closer to 50:50. This means that both parties have an equal share in the responsibility, the work and the benefit that comes with a good relationship.

opportunity to change and must take the initiative to do so in order to fit in to a new and better world. Good trainers help a weak horse become stronger, a tough horse to become sweeter and so on.

In *Think Like Your Horse* I explained in detail the importance of balance: not being too hard and not being too soft. If you are too hard a horse will resent you, on the other hand, if you are too soft, he'll exploit you. It's the principle of using as little as you need at every second. Never use less than you need to get the job done and never use more than you need to get the job done. Just as little as you need.

Over the next few pages I describe some of the types of horse I tend to encounter in my day-to-day work. You may recognize horses you know among them.

Anxious

These are sweet-natured gentle horses that basically try too hard and become anxious about making the wrong move. They're desperate to do the right thing but find themselves in conflict when it comes to making a decision. As they hesitate and switch from one possible decision to another, their head fills up with too many choices and as the deadline presses, they overload, often leaping frantically into a choice that may be right, but is often wrong. This frequently lands them in trouble, causing them to become more anxious about decisions they may make in the future.

working with this type
- Give this horse positive help with his decisions and guide him to succeed, while showing indifference to any mistakes he makes.
- Never reprimand him for mistakes, because if he is trying, but the trainer punishes him when he gets something wrong, then he will lose faith in his ability to get anything right and become fearful of the consequences associated with making the wrong decision, which in turn will make him more anxious in the future.
- The more successes this type of horse experiences, the more he'll believe in himself and the more he will relax with the training.

Workman-like

These are my favourite horses. Mostly mares, they are the tomboys of the horse world desperately trying to hide their femininity and putting on a tough exterior to be like the lads. They are a bit naughty but with a cheeky glint in their eyes and in lots of ways are more like a cheeky colt than a mare. They tend to be incredibly at ease with themselves and in control of their lives, never letting anything get in the way of their fun, while playing just inside the rules.

I like these mares because they are reliable. They look after themselves when they are ridden and also when they are out in the field. They rarely get injured and never get into an irrational panic about things. They give you as little as they possibly can but if you ask them correctly and enthuse them, they will give you everything and more.

working with this type
- Humour this mare through situations and make everything a game with her.
- Never try to confront her head-on, as she will tend to tough it out without even raising her pulse rate.
- Work as close to the 50:50 (see page 22) as you can because if you're too soft she'll just have fun with you but if you're too hard she'll be deliberately resistant and do less for you.
- A word of warning: if you choose to bully this type of mare, you may be able to be tough enough one day but she'll hold it against you the next and make you work even harder tomorrow.

Genuine young character

These are well raised and well socialized horses that have no hang-ups or preconceptions about people or new situations. They are comfortable that the world isn't a bad place but still have a healthy amount of scepticism. They understand their place in the world and how that relates to human beings. They don't panic and if something does worry them, they will seek advice from people. They are considerate of people and other horses and see themselves as only one part of the bigger picture. They have the confidence to voice their opinions but will always do so politely and still remain open to alternative suggestions. They are up front with their emotions and sensitive to injustice.

working with this type

- The most important thing with this type of horse is not to damage their enthusiasm by over-facing them with your goals.
- Don't push them too hard – this type will always get there in the end.
- Be prepared to adjust your approach so that you maximize on their good days and do less on the days when they are off form. It's all too easy to do too much with a horse that shows willing.

Cocky youngster

Generally between 6 months and 4 years, this type of horse comes into the barn thinking he owns the place, and has little or no respect for his surroundings or those in it. Typically, he is difficult to lead or to do most day-to-day tasks with, such as picking out feet, grooming and so on, and his behaviour is influenced more by mischief than anything else. You would expect this horse to attempt to intimidate his handler in the field – and often be successful at it, too – perhaps by trotting cockily towards them with his head and tail raised and showing no respect for personal space. He will either come bounding right over the top of you when you enter the field, or pass very closely kicking out as he goes. It's not aggressive behaviour but is more disrespectful and impolite.

When he is being led in hand, he will tend to be disruptive by not walking forward, nipping the handler's arm, nibbling the rope and so on. He may be bargy and try to pull ahead of you. When confronted, this type will take on the challenge confidently, often rearing playfully as though it were a game, almost delighted to have caused a reaction in the handler.

On one hand this is normal young horse behaviour and is perfectly acceptable when he is with other horses and, in fact, is a necessary part of a horse's social development. However, sometimes these types emerge where the horse has not been socialized correctly within a herd situation and has not been reprimanded by their mother or other herd members. Cocky youngsters are often overfed and generally over-indulged by their owners and have been given the benefit of the doubt too often.

working with this type

- This horse has got to learn that this behaviour is not acceptable when he is with people: they pay the bills and so must be listened to, respected and taken care of.
- It may be necessary to be a bit tougher on this type to bring the relationship back to a respectful 50:50.
- Any discipline you impose should be purposeful but not personal. Don't be harsh or raise your voice but simply make your point and when he responds make sure he knows you love him again to remind him that the 50:50 is where the relationship should be.

Lacking inspiration

There's a young lad who comes and helps me sometimes to do odd jobs around the place. He only comes when he feels like it and how much work I get out of him on a particular day depends on what sort of mood he's in. Sometimes he just wants the money and doesn't want to work for it. First impressions would suggest that he's lazy and yet when I give him a job to do that excites him, he works well at it, and when the job is completed he's obviously proud of his efforts.

Some of the difficulty is motivation. Potentially, he has a lot of ability and certainly has the intelligence to go far. He knows where he wants to be but he finds it difficult to get excited about the day-to-day stuff because he doesn't believe there is a connection between what he has to do today and where he wants to be in the future. There is also a kind of arrogance about him and a self-belief that is masking a deeper feeling of insecurity, which becomes clear when you get talking to him. He is worried about his direction but doesn't know who to ask for help. He doesn't want the responsibility of running things but doesn't trust anyone else to run them either. He's in desperate need of a role model who will direct him positively but direct him within his own parameters and at his own pace, but he has lost faith in those who have directed him in his past and blames them totally for the way things are now. He has come to the conclusion that doing nothing except what's necessary for his basic survival is better than doing the wrong thing.

I mention this lad because he reminds me of a particular type of horse I get in quite regularly. These horses have been broken and riding for two or three years but don't feel like they are moving on. To them, every day is the same and while it was exciting in the beginning, things have gone a bit stale.

working with this type

- Subtlety is the key thing here.
- Make things interesting without being patronizing and treating this type like a youngster.
- It is no good bursting into the barn with heaps of enthusiasm expecting this type to meet you on your level of enthusiasm. Instead you have to work from where they are and gradually build them to where you'd like them to be. In other words, let them amble to begin with then gently introduce things that may inspire them.

Nervous and sceptical

Nervous and sceptical describes the majority of horses before they begin training, or during the early stages of the training process. By nature horses are nervous and sceptical of new things and, as far as they are concerned, it is this scepticism that has helped them to survive as a species for millions of years. Being cautious in new situations and wary of new things is key to staying alive.

With a careful, fulfilling training schedule, most of this nervous scepticism will begin to disappear. However, many of the horses I see have somehow carried this attitude on into their training and are caught up in a cycle where they have become frightened of a part of the training process and can think of nothing else than to resist it by attempting to flee. It may be they are unhappy about saddling, bridling, long reining, mounting or anything in fact. Often the human reaction to the evasive behaviour is to assume that the horse is being naughty to get out of the work and so the person gets tougher on the horse. The consequences of this are that the horse becomes more nervous of people, tack, work, and becomes more evasive, which gets him into even more trouble. Obviously, this affirms in him that

the world is a scary place and that people are trouble and he becomes ever more nervous, working harder at ways to get out of his situation. Typically these horses will be difficult to catch, resistant to being tacked up and will appear (with good reason) unwilling to co-operate. They develop a heightened awareness of their surroundings, are often jumpy, find it difficult to keep on weight and so on.

working with this type

- As trainers, our job is to convince such horses that the world is not such a scary place and that it is possible to be a little bit more relaxed about life and still survive.
- It's all too easy to add to a horse's scepticism by presenting new things incorrectly. Therefore, when we present new things to this type of horse, or indeed any horse, we must be sure to ease them through the learning curve without ever over-facing them. This way we can lessen their fears of the world instead of adding to them.

Sad and depressed

I often come across horses that have been around for a few years – they're usually between 8 and 12 years old – and that appear to me to be what can only be described as sad or depressed. It's almost as though they're disappointed with how their lives have turned out, but at the same time are completely accepting of it with little initiative to change it. They are not angry or resentful but just seem to be in an inert state of being with very little energy or enthusiasm for anything around them. They tend not to socialize with other horses and show little affection for anyone or anything.

These horses rarely cause their owners trouble because they don't think beyond their own basic existence. It's like they've shut down to the outside world merely performing the duties they need to survive. They munch on their hay or graze in a field and take no notice of a horsebox arriving, for example, whereas other horses may trot to the fence to investigate. When you ask them to do something like move over in the stable they often take a moment to wake up to the possibility of an outside stimulus before eventually performing the task.

Many people are happy to own a horse like this because they're no trouble and can be used without the need for sensitivity on the owner's part. The downside is that they never reach anything like their full potential and appear to be more susceptible to injury, illness and disease. They are often described as characterless and yet you can imagine them with the spark and enthusiasm for life that all foals are born with.

working with this type

- Often these horses simply need kindness. With depression comes apathy and these horses have often been bullied into work.
- Break this cycle by helping these types to open up to you so that they can, in turn, become happier and then their work will improve. There is a big responsibility on us not to let them down once they have opened up.
- The difficulty many people have with horses is in managing their exuberance without suppressing it, as here, because while this might make the horse easier to handle, it also takes so much away from him.

The teenage phase

Teenage horses tend to be in the 2½ to 4 year age group (our equivalent of teenage). They make mistakes because they're trying things out – exploring the world through trial and error – not because they're trying to be naughty. For example, they might kick out or barge just because they're testing their boundaries. Teenagers tend to show all their emotions on the surface and are completely transparent and easy to read. They are, therefore, also sensitive to the outside world and will react positively or negatively, according to how they are treated.

working with this type

- A youngster like this needs careful work – this is when you make a good or bad horse. If he is not corrected at this stage, it will be harder for him to accept correction at a later stage.
- He will only need a tiny amount of correction because, although there may be plenty of attitude and opinion, there's no real conviction in what he's doing.
- Avoid being too hard on this type of horse: all he needs is a little bit of guidance. However, while it should be sympathetic, any correction must be successful, otherwise you might reinforce the wrong behaviour. Being too hard will toughen him up and cause resentment, while being too easy will allow him to realize he can do what he wants.

The trust fund horse

I seem to be seeing more and more of this type. Generally, they are well-bred horses that have been expensive to buy and are treated more like luxury cars than horses by their owners. Everything around and on them is polished daily and they sit very high up in the hierarchy of the human world. They are often viewed as more important than the farrier, groom, husband or anyone else involved with them, and nothing is ever their fault. All problems and potential hardships are resolved for them. As a result of this treatment, they have a kind of arrogant air and an indifference to the goings on around them. They have little or no concept of mutual respect and do not see themselves in context with others at all. As far as they are concerned, the world revolves around them and they genuinely can't see anything beyond their own needs. It's not their fault. It's simply what they have been led to believe over time, often from the day they were born. For example, they are often too precious to have lived out with other horses and as a consequence have never had any grounding 'reality check' from existing in herd life. Effectively, they have achieved a position of respect that they do not actually deserve and haven't earned.

working with this type

- Initially, this type needs to cease being the centre of attention. They often get attention from negative behaviour so at first their behaviour may get worse. When this fails they start to feel vulnerable and it's at this point that you can show them some genuine consideration. This will mean much more to them as they are experiencing a genuine need for the first time.
- It can be hard for these horses when they finally realize that respect is earned and not a birthright and that they actually have to do something good before getting appreciated.

Bottle-reared

Anybody who knows horses will tell you that horses that have been bottle-reared, or incorrectly imprint-trained, are horrendous to be around. They are not like horses at all. It is as though their senses are deadened and they seem to have no fear of the consequences of their behaviour, either for themselves or for others. However, they aren't really bold, but could be more accurately described as stupid, often getting themselves into scrapes with both horses and humans without learning how to avoid the same situation in the future.

In the early months of their life, people think these horses are perfect because they don't avoid contact with people as a normal foal would. They don't spook or panic and even appear to be quite cuddly. The trouble is that they are fine while they are doing what they want to do, and because we don't ask much of them in the early days, everything seems to be going well. The problems arise when you get further into the training process and need them to become more considerate of others. Because they are unconcerned about confrontation they tend not to care about finding a middle ground in which to work with people. They just want to do what they want to and will often turn to aggression to get their own way.

working with this type

- There are no hard and fast rules with these horses. They run along lines outside the bounds of horsemanship because they are effectively man-made.
- The horsemanship I have learned uses the horse's nature as a starting point and its almost like this has been bypassed to some degree or another in the bottle-reared or badly imprint-trained horse.

The trader

Many horses live their lives doing what they're expected to do rather than what they enjoy doing and see the interaction with people as a necessary evil rather than an enjoyable aspect of being part of the family.

Take this situation – you go to work and do what your boss tells you to do each day and in return you get your annual holiday and pay check at the end of the month. Would it be right for me to assume that you are happy in your work and enjoy your job? Or is it a possibility that you're just doing what you have to do to please your boss, just to get your pay before going home and then doing what you really love doing, whatever that may be. It is a sad fact that all of the clicker-trained horses I've met have this type of cold trading mentality about them, rather than the considerate sociable nature that they would have been born with. As humans, we know that pay is not enough on its own and we will work much harder for appreciation, provided it's genuine appreciation and not a contrived attempt at coercion. We should be the same in our interactions with horses. With such complex social animals simply trading on a deal-by-deal basis is not enough. Horses need to live and feel part of something closer than that.

working with this type

- When using clicker training, or any entirely reward-based system, it's essential to maintain the affection during the process so that it doesn't become mechanical.
- The relationship should be the priority with the goals being elements that are integral to the relationship and being something that will benefit each party.
- Horses have evolved into complex social animals and it is much more effective to appeal to them on an emotional level not just a material one.

2 Creating the 100% Horse

To create a 100% horse you have to begin by teaching him to stop and consider problems and look for solutions rather than to flee. Obviously, it is best to begin with small problems that a horse can solve relatively easily and build on these, so that he gradually learns to cope with bigger and more challenging problems that he might encounter in the future. It's important to begin this process in an environment where you are in control of such variables as the length of exposure, speed of the exposure and intensity of the exposure. It is not a good idea to attempt to do this work in a real-life situation to begin with, as in this situation much of what is going on around us is out of our control and if the horse becomes upset this will create a negative perception for the future and hamper further learning experiences.

The horse's CV

Take a few minutes to jot down all the things that you would look for in your perfect horse. The sort of things that you would like to see in a 'for sale' advertisement if you were thinking about buying a horse. Apart from being beautiful and being capable of performing well at dressage or jumping, or whatever your favourite equestrian activity, you would probably want a horse that seems to enjoy being around people and never gives you a moment of bother when you are doing the routine jobs that more or less every ridden horse has to accept, such as grooming, shoeing, tacking up and so on. Now think about your horse. Is he a

pleasure to be around? Do you have a good working relationship, or does he give you moments (or more) of worry or discomfort? The chances are that no matter how much you love your horse, there are things he does that you wish he wouldn't, or things he doesn't do that you wish he would. Often we are prepared to live with small irritations, but we don't have to. In fact, sometimes the small irritations are symptoms of larger problems that we really should be addressing. When you spend some time on improving the basic skills, you will find that your relationship with your horse improves in other areas as well.

basic skills

There are some basic things a horse has to be able to do not only to survive, but also to be useful to and accepted among people. Here is a basic job description for the horse. The 100% horse will do these things in all situations and under any conditions.

- **Lead easily,** walking nicely and not barging or pulling away (see page 44).

- **Tie up happily,** standing still and not pulling or fidgeting (see page 48).

- **Allow general handling** including allowing his front and back feet to be picked up and moved around (see page 50).

- **Stand quietly to be groomed,** without pulling faces, fidgeting or kicking (see page 54).

- **Accept his head being touched** (see page 55)

- **Accept being washed** and not be afraid of water or hoses (see page 58).

the micro-herd: building a partnership

As herd animals, horses feel more secure in groups. If there are other horses around your horse will be more inclined to follow them rather than rely on you. The challenge is to encourage your horse to place enough trust in you that he doesn't feel as if he's out there on his own. When he becomes troubled by something, he should understand that you are there for him and that you will help and bolster his confidence.

For this reason, I like to do as much one-to-one work with a horse as I can without support from other horses or riders. When it's just you and him, there is no other option but to work together, which is the state of affairs we want to achieve. The ideal is to reach a situation where you and your horse are interdependent, a kind of micro-herd.

more skills

So you think you have a good relationship with your horse? How good are you at opening gates, loading into a lorry or trailer, going through water, riding past spooky things, coping with livestock? These are more fairly basic skills that you and your horse can and should be able to cope with (see pages 84–129).

- **Stay alert and responsive to his handler** in the stable and outside, moving sideways, backwards and forwards softly and willingly when asked (see page 60).

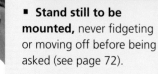

- **Be caught easily** (see page 66)

- **Be easy to tack up,** without resisting the saddle or bridle and having no fear of being girthed or bitted (see page 68).

- **Stand still to be mounted,** never fidgeting or moving off before being asked (see page 72).

- **Stand still to be clipped** without fear or resistance (see page 76).

- **Work well with long lines** (see page 74).

… and we haven't even started riding him yet!

There is a lot a horse has to learn, and often in a very short space of time, but none of these things is asking too much, and all of them are important to our relationship with him.

Planning your approach

Case study: the horse that didn't like being saddled

Whatever problem you have with your horse, it is important that you have a plan for how to deal with it. The first thing is to decide whether he is afraid and needs more support from you or whether he is being stubborn and deliberately difficult and needs keeping up to his job. This case study is about a horse that is worried about being saddled, but the principles and procedures are the same for most situations. Horses are very aware of your emotions, so think positively. Be constantly aware of the horse's perception of what you are doing. This is largely intuitive, but it is possible to determine what a horse is feeling and thinking by reading his body language, and taking into account his character type (pages 22–33). Choose a calm quiet day to work on the horse. You won't achieve anything when the odds are stacked against you, such as there's a gale blowing and rain pelting down, or there's too much distracting activity going on in the yard. Your horse needs to be relaxed and you can help him relax by, for example, walking him around on a halter or asking him to perform simple familiar tasks, which will reassure him. If such gentle manoeuvering doesn't work, it is possible that he is tense because of physical discomfort, which you will need to investigate.

STEP 1: Assess the problem

1 As I start to saddle this mare, she knows what's going on and she's a little wary, but I've allowed her freedom to express herself by giving her a long lead rope. Reassurance is vital at this stage.

2 I work briskly and quietly. Don't spend too long making adjustments, as this gives a horse time to think and she may decide that she's not going to allow whatever it is to happen.

3 I become aware that she is about to say, 'I can't cope.' I need to see her with the saddle on, so I tell her, 'Yes you can.'

4 Fast but smooth reactions are needed. The mare moves forward, which is much like saying, 'No I can't allow this', and I correct her because she's been doing the right thing up to now and I want her to realize that this is the easy thing to do.

prepare yourself

Choose a safe area to work in. Have all the equipment that you need for the job readily available, it is very distracting and spoils concentration to have to keep going off to search for bits and pieces. When you start work, be smooth but not creepy in your movements. Don't tiptoe around.

STEP 2: Physical checks

1 As this mare has an issue with the saddle, I ask Lesley to check her over for physical problems. There is usually a reason for a horse's behaviour, and Lesley finds that the mare is sore in her neck and around the wither area.

2 The problem extends along the mare's back, either side of the spine, to the lumbar region.

3 You can see from the horse's reaction that she doesn't like being touched where the girth goes. Lesley tells me that the mare's pectoral muscles are very tight and she would expect her to resent being girthed up.

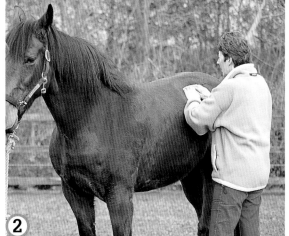

anticipation of pain

After a horse has suffered pain from a poorly fitting saddle, it is not enough to have a new saddle. The horse needs to be reassured that the saddle will not hurt. Once the saddle is on the horse's back, don't assume that he will not feel pain: anticipation of pain that is no longer there can be as real as pain itself.

relaxed or tense?

Indicators of relaxation include licking and chewing, flopping ears, generally relaxed musculature, soft smooth movements.

Signs of tension include a high head carriage, whites of eyes showing, a tight bottom lip, with the upper lip overhanging it.

4 If you think your horse's saddle may be causing problems, lunge her without any tack and observe how she moves. Then tack up to see if anything changes.

5 When the saddle is on, you can see how this mare's stride alters, becoming much shorter and more restricted.

6 Within a few seconds she is showing her discomfort even more extravagantly.

Further investigation of this mare shows that she is sore in the many muscles lying under the saddle. This is quite a common problem.

When we check the horse's saddle, it is too tight – you should be able to easily insert the length of your fingers between the horse and saddle and be able to move them down the front of the flap.

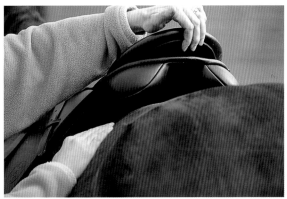

The back of the saddle also moves a great deal as it does not sit on the horse's back properly (see also below, left and right).

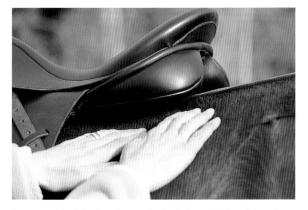

From the side, it is clear that the back of the saddle barely touches the horse. It should rest all along the back, which distributes the weight of the saddle and rider effectively over a wide surface.

You can see here that a finger's width can be inserted between the saddle and the horse's back, which again indicates a poor fit.

STEP 3: Addressing behaviour issues

Once we are sure that the saddle is no longer causing any physical discomfort, I begin to work through the mare's fear of being saddled. All the work is done simply and sympathetically.

1 The mare looks a little bit suspicious of what I am about to do. I've got the lead rope over my elbow, which I'm raising to bring her attention around to me. I touch her with my hand to increase her awareness of my presence.

2 At each step, I'm making the mare fully aware of what I am doing.

3 I do not try to trick her into having the saddle pad on her back. She has to accept each part of the process, otherwise it's not a genuine result.

4 You can see that her interest in what I am doing has increased – this also shows how relaxed she is about it. She is not tense, nor is she looking for a way out.

Repeating the process Consolidate what you've done by repeating the process but being a little bit quicker. Don't overdo it. School the horse to accept a more intense way of being saddled. Be more business-like.

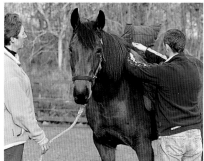

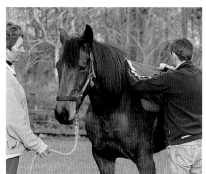

treat your horse sympathetically

Eventually, you can progress to putting on the saddlecloth and saddle. If your work has been successful, you will find that the horse accepts each stage and remains relaxed and happy throughout. If she is a little tense, repeat the steps, making sure that you gain her acceptance at each stage (see also 'moving and timing', below, to learn how to improve your approach).

moving and timing

If at this stage, a horse moves right away from you, you've overdone the work and haven't been sympathetic enough. If she moves away just a bit, make sure you move with her. Timing is vital – anticipate and move as she moves, as if the move was your idea. If you are late in moving, you will defeat the object: the horse will see it as a pursuit. Don't move too early – before the horse does – otherwise she will lose trust in you.

Easy to lead

To me, if a horse leads correctly it tells me that his mind is where it should be. If he stops when I stop and moves when I move at the pace and in the direction that I move, then I believe he understands the majority of what he needs to know about life with people. We humans are easily pleased by a horse who will listen to what we want and who comes willingly with us when we lead him up and who will stop and give us space to move around in a gateway for example. A horse that leads well shows an acceptance of his place in the human's world and also acceptance and trust in the people around him.

Leading is one of the first things I will teach a horse when he comes to me for training. In fact with every horse I work with I begin by checking that leading is in place before I go on to anything else. If you think about it, whatever you need to do around a horse you need to know that he is listening and will be polite and respectful of your space and thoughtful enough to move backwards, forwards, left and right when asked so that you can position him for the job in hand. These are basic manners.

When a horse is resistant to being led it can be for a number of different reasons. In young horses it can be because they don't know what they are supposed to be doing or don't understand the way they're being asked. When they feel the pull on the rope or somebody starts to hassle them, they feel trapped, get fearful and have to attempt to escape. In other circumstances it may be that a horse does know exactly what is being asked of him but is worried about something he sees ahead and has not got enough trust in the handler to help him through it. Then through fear he tries to escape the situation. There are also those horses that are simply being disrespectful and will pull away from a handler in order to get out of work or to get to a patch of grass they like the look of. So a horse that leads well shows us that he is trusting of the handler, is respectful of the handler, understands the communication being used and also understands his own responsibility for maintaining his position within the horse world.

1

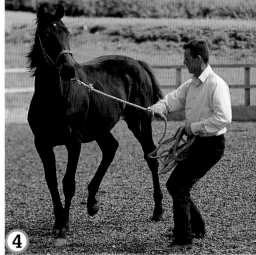

4

preparation

Before attempting to lead an unschooled youngster, teach him the basic principles of how to step towards you, to the left and to the right, so that he knows how to release himself from pressure and learns to have some respect for the headcollar. Do this work in a stable, to ensure it is safe and easy for him to make the correct move.

Teaching a youngster

This youngster is very definitely a cocky character (see page 26) and this sequence of me teaching him how to lead shows the importance of simple well-mannered leading. This type of unruly behaviour can be intimidating and could be dangerous. However, experience is one thing that youngsters don't have and there are not many moves in a young horse's repertoire. Most will try several things to get away from you – be prepared for those shown here – but they will exhaust their options quickly. Once a youngster is responding to basic requests from the lead rope, start teaching him how to walk along with you. Make sure he stops when you stop and walks when you do.

1 Thomas, the colt, rears outwards in an attempt to get away.

2 He then ducks around behind me and I turn around to correct him.

3 Finding his escape route blocked, he goes back around me and tries the other way.

4 He begins to realize that his antics are getting him nowhere.

5 To make it easy for him to do the right thing, I arc in front of him to get his shoulder moving; as soon as he makes a step, he gets some slack in the rope.

Retraining an older horse

It is important that leading work is done properly at a young age. Older horses who have not had good early training may learn that they can resist being led, which is irritating and can lead to problems in other situations, such as being tied up and loading.

This mature horse has learnt how to resist his handler, dragging backwards instead of moving freely forward (1). To get him walking I use a long lead rope to enable me to put some distance between us. This gives him the feeling of being left behind, which he doesn't like. He wants to move into the gap between us. It also gives me the freedom to move outwards in an arc that means he doesn't have to go far to get slack in the rope, which is his reward. In any situation where you are teaching a horse a skill, engineer opportunities for him to receive these little rewards. My aim is to have the horse come up alongside me in walk, and stop when I stop. I push him out to the side (2) because I want him to walk to one side of me, not behind me (3), otherwise he is in a position to run me over. Be prepared for the horse to become distracted and make sure you can do a turn to bring his focus back onto you. Then you can do something else, such as stop this way they will become aware of how important it is to keep their attention on you (4).

Key leading problems

Here are two leading problems that I commonly come across in my work. They can be very annoying, but are also relatively easy to overcome, so long as you remain sensitive and thoughtful, and don't get into a fight.

Leaning on the rope and dragging behind
What happens?
- The horse walks with you but leans on the rope and tries to drop in behind you.
- He plays with the rope, tries to get it in his mouth.

Why?
- Although this is not extreme behaviour, the horse is learning how to render the handler ineffective.
- He is not taking his work seriously because he hasn't understood his 50 percent responsibility in the human-horse partnership (see page 22).
- He is testing to see how strong he is compared to his handler so that he can use this to exploit other situations in the future. The next thing he may try in addition to this behaviour is planting himself to see what benefit this brings.

To overcome this situation

In a horse that is being stubborn in this way, I use what I've called the 'quarter loop' (see page 98). Because the horse has effectively gone dead and unresponsive to the headcollar, you need to motivate his movement and stimulate attention from elsewhere.

Stubborness isn't the only reason why a horse will hang back but it is the most common. Sometimes,

using the 'quarter loop'

The quarter loop (see page 98) is a loop in the end of a rope that fits over a horse's quarters. It is useful for getting a horse's back feet moving when he has planted himself. It is important to use it as a cue, and not to try to physically haul a horse into moving. I use it very much as a last resort for a horse who has stopped responding to the halter. Be careful how you put on the quarter loop and how you use it because some horses are more sensitive than others, and it may produce more forward movement than you can deal with. When used correctly it's an excellent tool, but if used too aggressively it will sensitize a horse to it and frighten him, and if used too softly it will be viewed as just another thing to resist or ignore.

overfacing your horse

It's incredibly easy to over-expose a horse and damage his confidence. The best way to avoid this is to spend every second you work with him trying to see the world through his eyes. This way you will tune into his perception and will be aware of potentially traumatic situations, avoiding them until he is ready to cope with them. Where a trainer presents a horse with a situation that he can't cope with, the horse will try to escape, and a battle ensues. If the trainer wins, the horse feels bullied and the relationship is damaged. If the horse wins, the trainer feels bullied and the horse loses respect. The key is to work together so that situations are overcome positively without losers.

especially with youngsters, you may find they are afraid of what is ahead and in this situation you have to be sympathetic and supporting so that they can trust you enough to walk up with you and get the job done. In this case I don't use the quarter loop but would encourage the movement by stepping the horse to the left and to the right to free up his feet. I call this 'bump-starting' because it brings a horse's focus forward and stops him from thinking backwards. With every step a horse makes towards you, show your appreciation with a rub on the head or neck.

Whipping around and pulling away
What happens?
- The horse spins away from the handler.
- He may pull the rope from the handler's hands.
Why?
- Some horses whip around and pull away because they are frightened.
- It may be that you've inadvertently put your horse in a situation that is too much for him and he hasn't got enough trust in you to help him through it.
- Sometimes horses whip round and pull away because they know they can get loose and out of work. This is very disrespectful and they know it.

To overcome this situation
If your horse is genuinely afraid the answer is to make things easier for him and remove the fear. It is essential not to get annoyed with your horse if he behaves like this because doing this will give him even fewer reasons to trust you, and make him feel more troubled. Instead

curing a headcollar bolter

Every time you walk your horse out to the field he barges past you, sets his neck and bolts over to his friends with the rope trailing. As you spend the next few minutes trying to catch him, you wonder why he couldn't have waited just a second more for you to let him free. The truth is he hasn't given it a thought; he's just doing this because it's what he does.

To overcome this situation
- Firstly, get a longer rope or a lunge rein instead of your normal rope. This way when he barges past you, you can keep hold of him and draw him back to you and let him go normally. This is often enough to break the pattern because most horses will just accept that this is the way things are.

- Another way of dealing with this situation is to have a kind of airlock system. Create a release area of about 6m x 6m (20ft x 20ft) just inside the gate, using electric tape. Again use the long lead rope and when he tries to escape from you, simply slip the rope until he meets the electric tape. This will stump him and he'll look round to you. Draw him back to you, give him a carrot or a rub on the neck, let him loose and open up a gap in the tape to allow him through. It's a simple way of breaking the pattern without resorting to force.

return him to something he is familiar with to build his confidence once again, then gradually work up to more testing situations, but this time taking smaller steps. With the horse that is simply trying to avoid work, you can be annoyed and should be. The trouble is that once a horse has seen benefit in this behaviour he may find it hard to forget and may resort to it in the future if the relationship goes out of balance. I call these horses headcollar bolters (see box above) and they are a nuisance to themselves and their owners. It almost becomes a pattern with them and often they repeat it just because it is what they did yesterday. The challenge is to break the pattern without resorting to a wrestling match. Horses are much bigger and stronger than us and fighting with them is pointless.

Happy to be tied up

There are many occasions when it is useful and important to be able to tie up your horse and be sure that he is comfortable and relaxed about it.

Tying up is an extension of leading. Leading teaches your horse what pressure on the halter means and he will have learnt to keep the slack in the rope so that he is not uncomfortable. He now knows that if his headcollar feels tight all he has to do is step forward to release the pressure, even though his immediate response might be to resist it. So when it comes to tying up to a solid object for the first time, in principle your horse should know the rules and know to step forward to release the pressure, not backwards to fight it. A major difference, however, is that when you are leading him, he has the benefit of your guidance and you will give and take to help him out. When he is tied to a solid object, there is no give and take, and it's possible that he may get worried about how this feels and fight it. To bridge the gap between leading and tying up, I use a long rope or a lunge rein on the headcollar. I pass this through the ring on the stable wall and then step away to the end of the rope. This way the horse is attached to the tying up ring but I still have the give and take needed to get him through the first stage. If he pulls back I can introduce a fairly solid feel to hold him to the ring while at the same time giving a little so as not to upset him. As he gets more comfortable with this, introduce a more solid feel to simulate what he would feel if he was tied up directly to the wall.

You can see when a horse has accepted this first part of tying up because when he steps back and the rope goes tight, he will correct himself by stepping forwards and returning the slack in the rope. When you are absolutely sure that he has understood this, you can tie him directly to the wall. It is common to tie a horse up to a piece of string, which will break (before the headcollar does) if something spooks him. This is a good idea but make sure the string is strong enough to hold a horse through a mild panic at very least because you don't want him to learn that he can break the string easily and go for a wander when he gets bored. I use baling twine with two different sized loops tied in it. If a horse pulls back against this, the small loop may give but the larger one will still hold him.

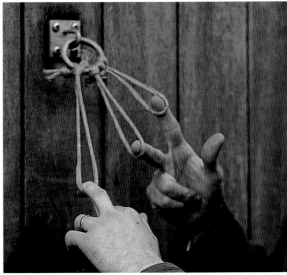

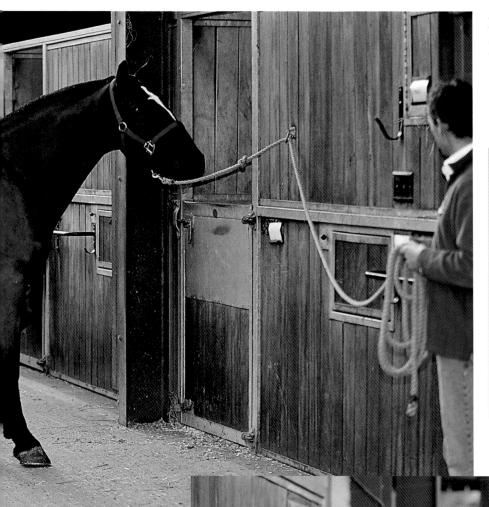

A long lead rope passed through a tie ring acts as a gentle introduction to being tied up.

safety note

Make sure the tie ring is secure and fixed to something solid that is not going to collapse before the baling twine breaks. I've seen occasions when a horse has been tied to a gate or fence, pulled away and taken the gate or part of the fence with them as they gallop around the yard.

You can make three or four loops (left) if you are expecting your horse to have more than one panic in a session but if you have done your preparation work first this should not be necessary (right).

Relaxed about being handled

A horse that allows general handling is showing a level of trust in people. Being touched and moved around by people is one of the things a horse has to accept, but it should be made as pleasant as possible. Once you have decided to work on this, you must continue even if at first he is resistant. Be firm and determined. Take the attitude that this job is going to be done today and that you wouldn't have asked if it was too much for the horse. At the same time, only do as much as the horse is capable of at any one time. For example, a young weanling can only accept so much in a day, but it is fair to increase what you ask of him as he becomes more experienced. Take into account the horse's character: a bolshy cocky youngster should be asked to put up with more, and may require more directness.

Co-operative with his feet

Feet are very important to the flight animal, so horses are naturally precious about them. The better condition a horse's feet are in, the faster he can run from trouble, and obviously we need to be able to handle their feet so that we can keep them in good condition too. The old saying 'no foot no horse' is so true, and unless a horse allows us to pick up and examine his feet he is jeopardizing his future. Apart from anything else when he finally allows his feet to be handled, it shows a huge leap of faith on his part and further reinforces his acceptance of the horse/human partnership.

Working towards trimming and shoeing

Once a horse has accepted the basic handling of feet he must then learn to accept more advanced handling. For example when the farrier comes he will want a horse to hold his feet in many different positions so that he can work on them more easily. With the front feet, the farrier will want to grip them between his knees so that he has his hands free to rasp around and nail on a shoe. He will also need to pull the front feet out forwards to rest them on a tripod so that he can clinch up and rasp around to finish off. With the back feet a farrier will expect a horse to hold his foot quite high so that he can rest it on his knees and have his hands free for rasping and nailing on. Likewise he'll need a horse to allow a hind foot to be pulled forward to a tripod so that he can clinch up and rasp around to finish off. Teaching a horse this advanced handling of feet before you book the farrier's visit is essential. Farriers are often very busy and have not got time to school your horse for you.

how not to do it

This owner is demonstrating the wrong way to pick up a hind foot. Although she is following conventional guidelines and putting her arm around in front of the leg and lifting from the inside, she has not warned the horse that this is what she is going to do. Instead, she's dived straight down to only just below the hock. In addition, this position is too high to pick up the foot, which means that it is not secure in her hand. As she leans in to pick up the horse's foot, her own foot leaves the ground, which would have the effect of unbalancing her should the horse resist in any way.

When I pick up a hind foot, I start on the quarters **(1)** and run my hand down the whole leg to the fetlock **(2)**. I make sure I am balanced evenly on both feet before I begin, so I can help the horse balance should he need it. Remember it is not 'natural' for horses to pick up their feet in this way; they don't automatically know how to balance. Youngsters in particular need help with balance.

I ask the horse to lift his foot, when my hand is at the fetlock **(3)**, which is a more secure area for him. Once the foot has come off the ground, it may need to go straight back down, so keep it low making it is easy for the horse. If you are happy that the horse is coping well, walk the foot back so that it makes a natural arc **(4)** to the position where a farrier might need it to be – the further backwards it goes the higher it comes.

Learning to lift his feet

In this sequence, I am increasing what I expect the horse to cope with in preparation for a farrier's visit. When this work is done slowly and progressively your horse will learn that there is nothing to be scared of and nothing to resist.

As with the back feet, start high – here on the nearside shoulder **(1)** – running your hand along the back of the horse's leg over the tendons and down to the fetlock. Once a horse is comfortable with that pick the hoof up and tap it. Progress to the nailing on position **(2)**, then pull the foot forward to clinching on position **(3–4)**. On the nearside, do this by passing the foot to the left hand and backing yourself around under the horse's neck. Keep the leg relaxed, don't pull it into position. Force will unbalance the horse and once this happens you have to let go, which is detrimental to the learning process. A horse with an established problem may pull even if you keep everything soft. If this is the case, don't let go, wait until he stops pulling – at this point you have a second or two's grace while he thinks about pulling again. This is the exact time to put his foot down, gently and briskly. He will have no reason to pull and he is getting the reward for stopping pulling.

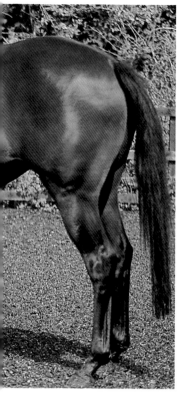

The aim is to be able to pick up both front feet and move them around relatively freely above the ground. Remember to do this work on the back feet, too, bringing them up **(5)** and forward **(6)** in the way that a farrier would.

Good to groom

Grooming is one of the most important things we can do for our horse. Apart from being good for his skin, coat and general health, grooming also allows us to examine him for cuts, lumps and other possible problems and when accepted and done well acts as a gentle massage to relax him and reward him for being in our company. Most horses like being groomed but some don't. This might be because they are 'thin-skinned', which means they are sensitive to the bristles of the brush and will pull faces or kick out at the handler. If you persist in brushing a horse that hates it, you can cause him to develop a life-long negative perception of grooming. It is, however, something a horse should learn to accept and even thin-skinned horses can begin to enjoy it, if it is presented correctly. Other horses that dislike grooming may be perceiving it as an imposition and feel that their privacy is being invaded. This is only the case when there hasn't been enough time spent building a relationship between horse and handler to create the necessary familiarity. Once a horse gets to know you, he will be more co-operative about grooming. Think of a situation where horses are turned out in a field together for the first time. They will spend a bit of time playing and getting to know each other first and eventually may engage in mutual grooming. This depends on how they get along with each other; some field companions rarely groom each other. Remember, then, that grooming is an intimate activity and we must make friends first before engaging in it.

The relationship is more important than anything, so don't sacrifice it for the sake of having your horse shiny. If he is to be worked, a horse will need to learn to stand to be groomed and the way it is introduced counts.

Begin with a soft brush or even a soft cloth or a sponge and work gently in areas that are not too intimate. I like to begin on the neck and work my way back to where the saddle sits and then onto the top of the quarters.

Don't do the head, belly or legs until you have first established acceptance in the neck, saddle and rump areas.

Accepts his head being touched

When it comes to bridling it is essential that your horse is not fearful or resistant about having his face and head touched; there are few things worse than a horse sticking his head in the air while you fumble around trying to bridle him. Apart from irritating us, it often causes the horse trouble too, and not just with bridling. Often we need to open a horse's mouth to dose him with wormers or check his teeth. We may need to

check his ears for mites or trim his poll. For these reasons, it's important a horse learns that he can allow a person into this area without being hurt or endangered. As we know, horses are naturally sceptical and particularly so around their head. A horse that allows his head and ears to be handled shows a good deal of trust and is beginning to understand the horse/human partnership.

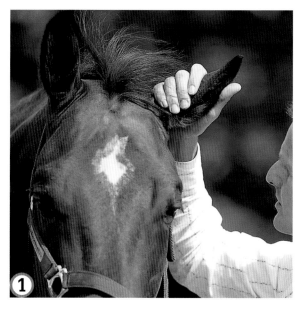

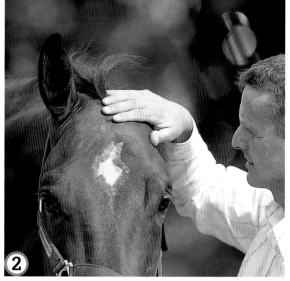

1–2 This horse is learning that it can be quite nice to have his ears stroked. When I introduce this concept, his head raises a bit **(1)**, but soon he's more relaxed **(2)**. The key is not to teach him that he can raise his head to get rid of your hands. Always work below that occurrence, perhaps by starting with an area that you know he is happy to have touched, such as the centre of his forehead. Work on both sides.

3 I follow a similar procedure to teach a horse how to accept handling in and around his mouth. In day-to-day handling of horses, it is vital to be able to check teeth and give wormers. Put your thumb in the corner of his mouth where there is a gap between the incisors and premolars so the horse can't bite you. Encourage him to 'mouth' like he would a bit. You could use this work to teach him a cue to open his mouth for bitting, such as gently pressing on the side of his mouth. Check for wolf teeth by running your finger along the side of the premolars.

Learning to lower his head

As with any other work, a horse needs to learn how to give to pressure in this area and lower his head when asked. Don't simply rush up and push down on the poll to bring down on his head. The horse needs to be relaxed first. If he is not, there is a danger that he will learn that he can simply put his head up to get out of reach, which is an evasion.

I introduce the horse to the concept of lowering his head by moving it gently side to side **(1–3)**. This motion releases the muscular brace in his neck, which encourages him to drop his head. As soon as he brings it down even slightly he gets a release, and in this way I am establishing a cue for lowering. It is important to repeat the work on both sides **(4)**. As with most handling work, the key is to ask the horse to give you something, when he does, even if it is only a small give, release, allow him a few moments of relaxation **(5)** and then ask for a little bit more **(6)**.

1

a headshy horse

Work even more slowly with a headshy horse, but don't be painfully slow as this will make him worried and restless. Stand out in front slightly so he can see you with both eyes. Begin working along the neck until he is comfortable with being touched all the way up the neck. Make sure that at each step you touch and come away, gradually extending the time you have contact with his body and then the size of the areas that you touch.

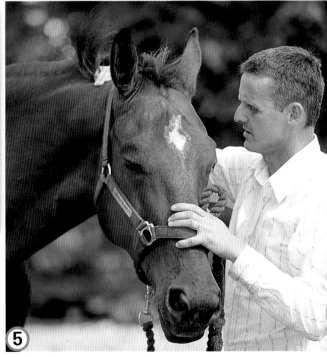

5

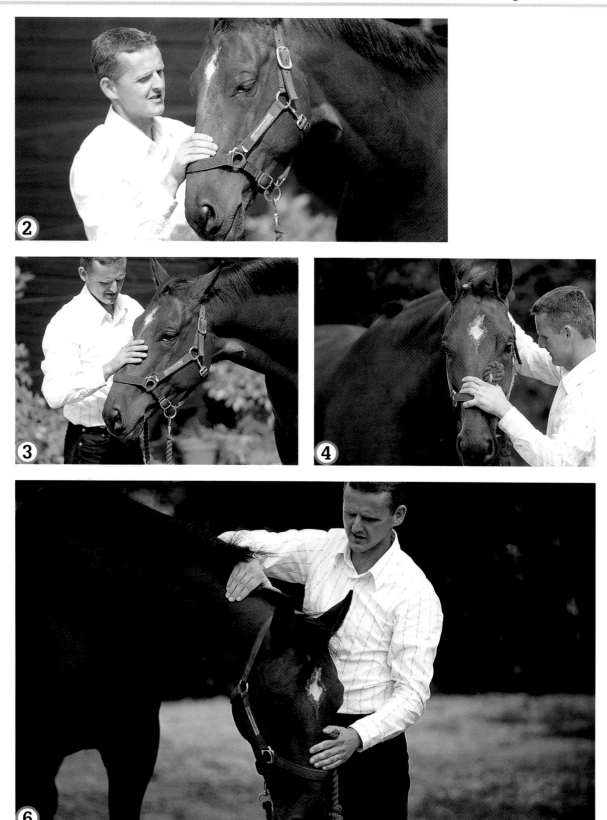

Laid-back about being washed

Although most of us don't make a regular habit of bathing our horses, when you do need to wash down a horse, for whatever reason, it is much easier if he already knows and accepts all that this involves. When you start to accustom a horse to washing, remember that a hose can be frightening if he has not seen one before and that, unless it is a lovely warm day, cold water is not going to be very welcome.

Be sympathetic to the horse's natural reluctance but remind yourself that you are not expecting too much of him and that this is a comparatively simple and straightforward skill for him to learn at this stage. Start teaching your horse to accept washing using a dry sponge around his head and neck. Expect him to raise his head initially but eventually aim to achieve the same relaxed attitude that you had with lowering the head (see pages 56–7). If need be, begin with a smaller sponge or a small cloth. When he is happy with a dry sponge dampen it and repeat.

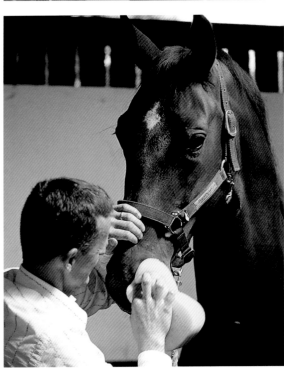

washing tips

1 Don't tie up your horse for washing. Instead have a long hose with plenty of slack so that you can move freely.
2 Do this work in a safe environment and hold both the horse and the hose yourself.
3 I find that a helper will tend to take over directing the horse, which means that you lose control of her movement. It is important to have this control as you can be instantaneous with your reactions, instantly making it more uncomfortable for her to move than to stay still and enabling her to realize that moving doesn't achieve anything.

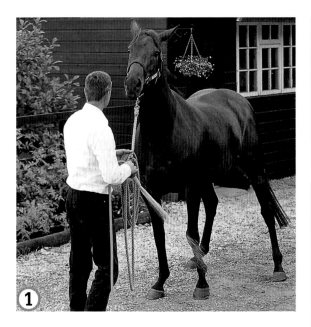

be active

When you are using the hose, be prepared to move around with the horse. If, say, he moves away as you bring the hose down to knee or hock level, go with him. Get your timing right so you don't pursue him (see page 43) but don't allow him to reward himself by getting away from the water.

For hosing, it is important that you have an adjustable nozzle on the hose and that you use a gentle jet **(1)**. I have found that horses really dislike a dribble of water and, in any case, it won't do the job. Introduce the water up high on the horse's body, for example on the shoulder or top of the foreleg if the intention is to get to the feet **(2)**. Generally, horses are happier if you start higher and work downwards. Establish that the horse is comfortable with what you are doing with each area of the leg before moving downwards **(3–4)**.

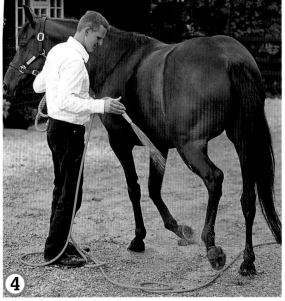

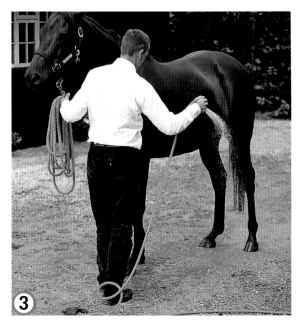

Alert to his handler

A horse that is prepared to move around and away from you readily, willingly and gently is a joy to be around. All sorts of tasks and care routines, from mucking out the stable to putting on rugs and tack, are made easier if your horse is aware of you and happy to react calmly to any requests you make of him. This sort of soft attentiveness work also has a positive effect on a horse's reactions when you ride him.

1 When you start training a horse to work around you, the priority is to teach him how to back away from you. This is because the most common evasion to a request for lateral movement is for the horse to walk forward, so you have to establish control over forwards and backwards movement before you can move a horse laterally.

2 The horse should move back from the tiniest suggestion from you. Ask him to move back either with a touch, from headcollar or on hand with chest, or a step towards him or use body language with a more advanced horse. If a horse challenges you, you need to up the level of pressure, gently but firmly reiterating your cue. There is no reason why he should not step back when you ask; it is a perfectly reasonable request.

3 This horse is quite resistant and bolshy towards me. He is making out he's worried and nervous about being asked to move. But in reality he just doesn't want to do it.

Moving laterally

Once I have him backing up responsively, we can progress to moving laterally, which I ask for by stepping up to his right shoulder from the nearside. Because I've established backing up, I can achieve sideways movement by first asking for a step back and then using this movement to get a step right by moving his head over to the right **(1–2)**. Moving the horse's head to the right will make him move his already moving foreleg (near foreleg) over to balance himself, which makes a sideways movement **(3)**. I want the near fore to cross behind the off fore, backwards and over, rather than forwards and over. I don't want to have to move my position to enable him to move over. He is moving quite lightly although he doesn't appear to be so **(4–5)**.

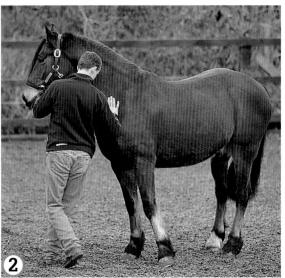

1

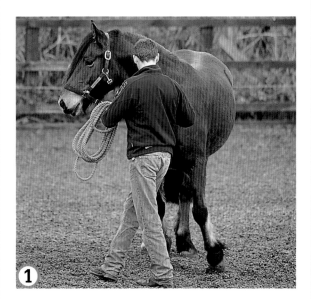

2

3

4

5

①

1 Finally, we work on moving the quarters over. It makes sense to work in this order as the most difficult direction for a horse to go is backwards, then next in difficulty is moving the shoulders sideways and the easiest, apart from going forwards, is moving the quarters sideways. The horse now knows how to go backwards and sideways from the front (see pages 60–63), which means that when I ask him to move his quarters around, he won't think he should come forwards and over me. He will find moving his quarters easy now that I've established the other skills.

2–3 I step along his nearside to his shoulder, which will stop him moving his shoulder left, then I bring his head around to the left and raise my rope coil with my right hand to ask him to move over. If my body wasn't asking him to stand where he is, he might try to move his shoulder towards me, but as it is he has to move his quarters away. Through the backing up work we've established that he shouldn't move forwards unless he's asked, so I can ask him not to move forwards with my left hand if necessary.

Easy to catch

One of the most frustrating things that can happen to a horse owner is having a horse that won't be caught. The horse always seems to know when he is going to be asked to work and that makes him doubly reluctant to catch. Using a tidbit such as a carrot is not really a satisfactory solution as the horse learns to take it and walk off before you've got the headcollar on, so it just teaches him that he can have a treat and still not be caught. From a human's point of view, this behaviour seems to be deliberately irritating. However, sometimes we have taught the horse not to be caught. He thinks that when he sees you coming into the field with a headcollar, you are there to chase him around, and so he obliges.

2 There is another horse in the paddock and this is a strong distraction to the youngster we are trying to catch. I have the owner bring this horse over to us, to bring the focus back to a smaller area. By arcing around the horse I prevent him turning his quarters towards me, which is how he usually gets control. This draws his attention back to me – he is virtually moving his front feet. It is vital not to get into the situation where the horse knows that he can get away. Either retreat or, while you still have his attention, arc around in front of him, still facing him and keeping him facing you. He will follow you with his head, and he might follow to some degree with his feet. As you keep his attention on you so you have the opportunity to decrease the distance between the two of you.

1 This owner is clearly demonstrating the chasing technique. She is approaching the horse head on in what he sees as a fairly threatening manner, so he turns to the right with his quarters to put her behind him, and give himself room to escape. This puts the owner behind him, which makes her a pursuant and puts her at a disadvantage. She continues to pursue the horse along that line, until he gets clear of her and then she realizes her predicament. In fact, from the horse's first move the situation is irretrievable so she should have abandoned it sooner. With a horse that is difficult to catch, always approach from in front but keep a careful eye on his attitude: if he looks like he's about to seek an escape, stop approaching and stop thinking of catching him.

3 As a horse becomes more comfortable, he
will reach forward to sniff you. It is important
the horse reaches forward to you rather
than you reaching forward to him. This is
simply generating interest: don't try to grab
the headcollar, it won't work, generate
interest instead. Approach the neck or the
slope of the shoulder, between the withers
and the top of front leg, and once you have
established contact and the horse is relaxed,
back away by a stride or two, then approach
that position again, extending the contact
time and eventually the contact area. Keep
thinking that you are training the horse to be
caught, not that you have to catch him. Once
you have established contact and the horse
becomes more comfortable, only then can you
make a move to clip on your lead rope. You
could then unclip straightaway and approach
again, or walk a few steps on the lead rope,
unclip and repeat. It is often your approach
that the horse needs to overcome.

Good to tack up

In my work with remedial horses, I always tack up without tying up the horse because I want him to have the option to stand with me or to move away. In other words, I want him to learn to stand and be tacked up because he is responding to what I've asked him to do, rather than because he can't do anything else because he is restrained by a rope and a ring on a wall. It's a good test to see where you are with a horse emotionally and it also gives the horse the opportunity to tell you if his saddle is uncomfortable or he's having back trouble or perhaps not liking the work or the way you ride. Presuming that everything fits correctly and your horse is absolutely comfortable physically, you can go about teaching him the discipline of standing still.

All horses, particularly youngsters, get distracted by things – perhaps a grass verge beckoning or the excitement of another horse leaving the yard – but whatever it is, he needs to learn that while you are working around him he must listen to your direction and nothing else. He must realize that what you ask of him is important to you and for him too. When you ask him to step half a stride forwards or backwards to position him for the saddle, he should do so without evasion. It's the same with the bridle. He should lower his head and open his mouth for the bit to make it easy for you both.

Bridling

This is the basic procedure that I go through to put on a bridle. It is simple and sympathetic, and by working this way I can see where a horse may need some additional schooling to be happy with what he is being asked to do.

1 Check that the horse is willing to lower his head for bridling. (See also pages 56–7.)

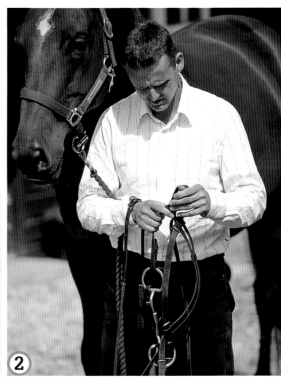

2 Adjust the bridle so that it is bigger than it needs to be and will go in his mouth and over his head without being uncomfortable.

tips for bitting

1 With a horse that is reluctant about bitting, generate his interest in the bit by allowing him to take it and then dropping it out again, gently, then the horse will begin to look for the bit.

2 Co-ordinate your left and right hand so that you can lift the bit into the mouth raising the headpiece with your right hand and present the bit with your left hand. Aim for a smooth movement to avoid banging his teeth.

3 With a horse that plays with the bit, make sure that whatever he grabs is the bit. Then reward him for this. This is an evasion or a playful thing – he is trying to disrupt the lesson.

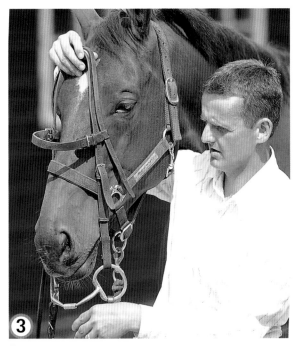

3 Check to see how your horse responds to the bridle in front of his face, without even trying to get the bit in his mouth. Only proceed to bitting if he remains soft and comfortable through this stage.

4 Cradle the bit in the palm of your left hand, if you are bridling from the left side, and then position it between his lips at the front of his mouth, using your thumb in the corner of the mouth to encourage him to open it. Don't bump his teeth or force the bit between his teeth; wait until his mouth is open before you lift the bit up and bring the bridle over his ears.

5 Once the bit is in the horse's mouth use your right hand to lift the headpiece over the offside ear and then your left hand to lift it over then nearside ear. (Adjust the various pieces to fit the bridle to the horse's head. Make sure that the bridle is clean and supple to begin with.) Make sure the horse is comfortable by pulling the mane and forelock gently into place. The whole experience should be reasonably pleasant for the horse.

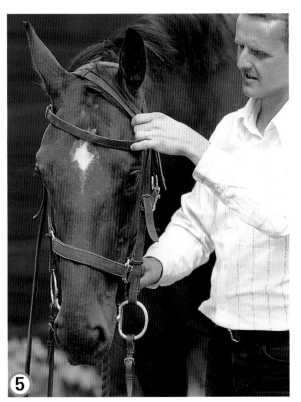

working on the 50:50 relationship

It's true that not having a horse tied up gives him more opportunity to evade you, but it also gives you more opportunity to correct and educate and reinforce the 50:50 balance in your relationship. Relationships must be dynamic and not static. Tying a horse to a wall is a static situation leaving no space for communication.

Saddling

As I am saddling up in an open space, I have the horse on a loose rope so he could move if he wanted to; this is deliberate because the horse has had problems in the past and needs reassurance that what I am doing won't hurt. For this work, I always prepare the saddle beforehand, fitting the girth onto the saddle and making sure that girth buckles on the offside are in a low enough position that the girth will fit around the horse without fuss. I then place the girth over the seat of the saddle in readiness.

1–5 Before you put the saddle pad on, make sure you have the horse's attention towards you on the nearside, and hold the pad ready in your right hand with your hand in the middle of it, so that it won't flick around when you place it over the horse's back. Stand just in front of his shoulder with your left forearm and hand in contact with his neck as a reassurance and to prepare him for the feel of the saddle pad. This will give him confidence. Put the pad on in one smooth movement so it is more or less even on both sides, almost on the withers. If your horse moves away at this point, keep contact and move with him. By moving with your horse, you make him realize that moving doesn't achieve anything, because he can't put any distance between you and him. Once he comes to a standstill, adjust the pad to its correct position forward and back and left and right. You could choose to repeat the process to consolidate the lesson or if you feel he is happy, continue to the next stage.

6 Pick up the saddle by putting your right forearm from the cantle forwards, so that the gullet rests along your forearm. This means that when you want to put the saddle on the horse you literally lift your forearm and put it on the horse's spine, then slide your forearm out.

7 Ease the numnah into the gullet. Go around to the offside and ensure the girth hangs correctly on the offside. It should hang no less than a couple of centimetres from the ground, which will ensure that it reaches around comfortably onto two holes on the girth billets on the near side.

2

3

taking care

When I am working with a youngster or an unknown horse, I girth them tight enough for the saddle to stay in place then unclip them to see what will happen, moving them off in walk, trot and canter. Don't assume that a horse will not react in any way.

5

8

8 Come back to the nearside and gently do up the girth tight enough that the saddle stays there whatever reaction you get, but not too tight and restrictive. Remember that if a girth is too loose the saddle pad could come out when the horse moves, then the saddle will be very loose.

7

Stands still to be mounted

It should never be necessary for somebody to hold your horse for you to mount. A horse should take responsibility for holding himself in position for the rider to mount, whether it's beside a mounting block, fence or in the middle of a yard. Whatever your preferred method of mounting, your horse should oblige. It's also important that he learns to remain standing once you are mounted so that you can get comfortable and make the necessary adjustments for riding, such as tightening of the girth and adjusting stirrups. Only when asked by the rider should he take the first steps forward.

Obviously in return we must be aware that our horse may become unbalanced or unsure as we mount, and we must make sure we don't poke him with our toe as we get on, pull him off balance or jab him in the mouth. Our responsibility is to make it easy on our horse by choosing a suitable method of mounting, so that we do not fumble around him and cause him to fidget.

Using a mounting block is by far the best way of getting on a horse for most riders and if the in-hand work has been done correctly beforehand then positioning a horse will be quite easy. Stepping up onto a horse from the ground isn't ideal for horse or rider but a horse should still learn to accept this way of mounting so that you are able to mount him while out on a hack or in the middle of a school or field.

If a horse is very restless when being mounted, it is as well to check that there is no physical problem that leads to apprehension about being uncomfortable when a person is on board. The problem may not be in the horse's back or even in the saddle fit, so get expert help if necessary.

keep him on the move

Never let your horse succeed in bringing matters to a halt when mounting; always keep him on the move, otherwise his behaviour will be rewarded. With a suitable mounting block, an alternative to moving the horse to and fro is to turn him around the whole block each time he attempts to swing out his quarters.

a typical mounting problem

This owner is illustrating a typical mounting evasion. She leads the horse to the mounting block and he happily follows her, but as she makes her move to pull him up nearer, he swings his bottom out. She gets off the block to reposition him again – a common reaction – and he looks like he's going to walk up just fine… but the cycle repeats again because the horse has learnt how to stop the mounting process from occurring. He doesn't mind repeating this a hundred times as long as it ends in him not being ridden.

1 A way to diffuse the classic evasion situation and discredit the horse's theory about mounting is to bring the mounting block out into a larger area where there is room all around it, and approach it in exactly the same way as before. When the horse tries his trick, I hold my position on the mounting block and hassle him...

2 ...as he swings his quarters out, I pull his head sharply to the right, he wants to avoid having his quarters near me so swings them around putting himself in the perfect position for me to bring him back around to the mounting block. I might need to do this several times but as soon as he starts to have his quarters in a more acceptable position, he will get a reward – no more hassle and a gentle pat. I don't mount him yet.

3 Now he is more thoughtful about what happens if he does the wrong thing and knows about the reward for doing the right thing, he is less likely to do the wrong thing.

4 All I am aiming for at the moment is for the horse to stand in position by the mounting block. I'll make no attempt to mount him at this stage, only when this good behaviour is established do I make a move to gather the reins for mounting.

5 With some horses, gathering up the reins, or placing a foot in the stirrup is a cue for them to move off. In each of these cases, use the same principles to

school him out of the desire to move. Remember to reward him when he is right and hassle him when he is wrong.

6 My preferred way of mounting with a mounting block is to lean over, so that my centre of gravity is in front of the saddle, before putting my left foot in the stirrup. This is to avoid pulling on the stirrup or on the side of the horse, which is kinder and it also gets rid of the trigger that makes the horse to move when you put your foot in the stirrup.

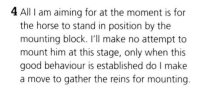

Experienced with long lines

Long lining is a good way of teaching any horse, old or young, to move forwards. It helps a horse develop a topline and can be used to introduce him to difficult situations and new experiences that you don't want to ride through. Long lining helps a horse become even in his paces before being ridden or after being off work for a while, particularly through injury.

I like to start off a horse long lining in a round pen for several reasons. When you start this sort of work inexperienced horses tend to want to run forwards; if you are in a round pen all they will do is go around in a circle, but in a big school you have to stop them doing this by pulling, which hurts their mouth and tightens up their quarters, and makes them run even faster. Also,

if you have to let go in a large arena the reins are left trailing, which can be dangerous.

I always connect the long lines onto the bit. I see no point in using a headcollar as I want to produce the responses in the horse's mouth. In a round pen where you don't have to pull, he can run and then come back to you without damage to his mouth, then he will settle down and start to learn feel. Be honest about your own ability here, it is only bad hands that spoil mouths.

Have the stirrups down and held in place under the belly with an old leather or similar strap. Pass a long rein though the nearside stirrup forwards from the horse's back end, and clip it to the nearside bit ring. From the nearside, pass the clip of the second long rein over

tips for controlling movement

1 If the horse gets 'stuck' send a pulse along a rein, both reins or scuff up some sand.

2 If you want to change directions, step out in front of the movement and he should turn away.

3 Never let the horse turn in towards you as this will tangle the reins.

the seat of the saddle until it touches the ground on the offside – this should be the correct length to pass through the offside stirrup and clip onto bit ring.

Return to the nearside, and step back from the horse to an angle of about 45 degrees, into a driving position. I keep the offside rein over the saddle at this point. I don't like to flick it over the horse's quarters as this

could be too much of a surprise with an inexperienced horse. Letting the reins slip through your hands, allow the horse to go off into a walk until he reaches the side of the pen, which will guide him around. Continue to have the reins slack, the offside one still going over the seat. After a few circuits, the horse might start think about making a turn. When he makes that move, allow him to do it, but ensure that he does it by turning away from you, so that the outside rein becomes the inside rein. Allow the outside rein to stay down over the hocks at this point, as it will naturally be there. At this stage, the pen is doing most of the work of keeping the horse going gently in the right direction. Work on both reins and then start to take a feel on the reins. The goal is to achieve smooth flowing paces and smooth transitions over as many days as you need. Aim for softness and calmness. Also work on stop and rein back. If you like you can work on associating voice commands.

Progress to long reining around a small paddock, where you can get in behind the horse to long line him. This is a good way to get out and about, with the horse learning to listen to you through his mouth.

Happy to be clipped

Although many horses can manage very well without being clipped, it is good to know that your horse will be relaxed about it should you need to clip him for any reason, or if his routine changes so that clipping becomes more of a necessity. In addition, a horse that will allow such a personal and relatively invasive procedure is showing a high level of trust in his owner and this will be of benefit in other areas of your relationship.

Case history

This 13-year-old horse had always had trouble being clipped and always had to be doped before he would accept the clippers. In this sort of situation, you only have one chance to get it right – if the horse starts to panic and the adrenalin kicks in, he will lose the ability to think about what you are asking in a logical way.

1 The owner demonstrates how she might try to clip the horse. She has simply turned on the clippers and the horse has been taken by surprise and tried to run away. Many people would do the same thing, not considering that what they are doing looks quite aggressive from the point of view of the horse.

2 As the owner makes her approach, he backs off even further. He perceives this as being pursued by something life-threatening.

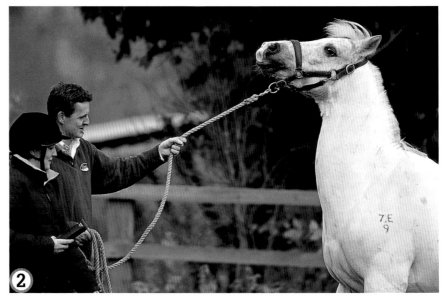

3 When I start working on the horse, the first thing I do is to angle my body so that I'm being less direct and less threatening to him; compare this with the previous photographs (1–2), where the owner is much more face on and does look quite frightening. I've also removed some pressure by working on my own. Without the second person, the situation is more of a one-to-one and so more balanced.

4 I want this horse to succeed, and therefore I make sure that my approach is sympathetic and unlikely to give him a negative perception of the situation. I move slowly with the clippers running, but held beside me not in front.

5 Once the horse realizes that I'm here to help him overcome his fear, he considers working with me. With horses that are phobic about the clippers it is important that the approach is sensitive but progressive, and that you take every opportunity to reward at regular intervals.

(continued overleaf)

6–8 Obviously, the aim is eventually to touch the horse's body with the clippers, but to show sensitivity I break this down into smaller steps. An important thing to note in this process is that each step is fragile and that one step is building one on top of the last, rather like a pyramid of cards. Always work with the understanding that a wrong move could cause the whole thing to collapse. For this reason, it is important to take small steps not trying to progress too quickly, which could jeopardize the work you have already done. When I'm starting to make contact, I do this at the shoulder, as horses seem to find this the least vulnerable area, and I always start by touching the horse with my left hand and then with the clippers.

9 Eventually I will extend the lesson to more vulnerable areas around the head and throat, legs, and flanks, again maintaining a sensitive approach.

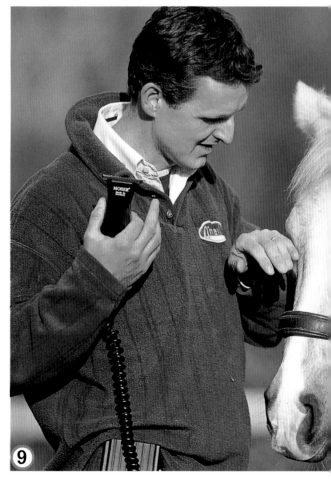

reward the right thing

In clipping, as with all horse work, it is vital to reward the right behaviour. All too often when the horse is worried by the clippers, we turn them off, which inadvertently rewards the wrong behaviour and teaches the horse that fleeing the situation is beneficial to him. We need to reverse the process and teach him that standing still considering solutions to the problem is the best thing to do. In other words, when we approach with the clippers and he makes a conscious decision to think about what we are doing, we can reward him for this by switching off the clippers and retreating for a few seconds. In this way a horse learns to stop, think and look for a solution, rather than to run away.

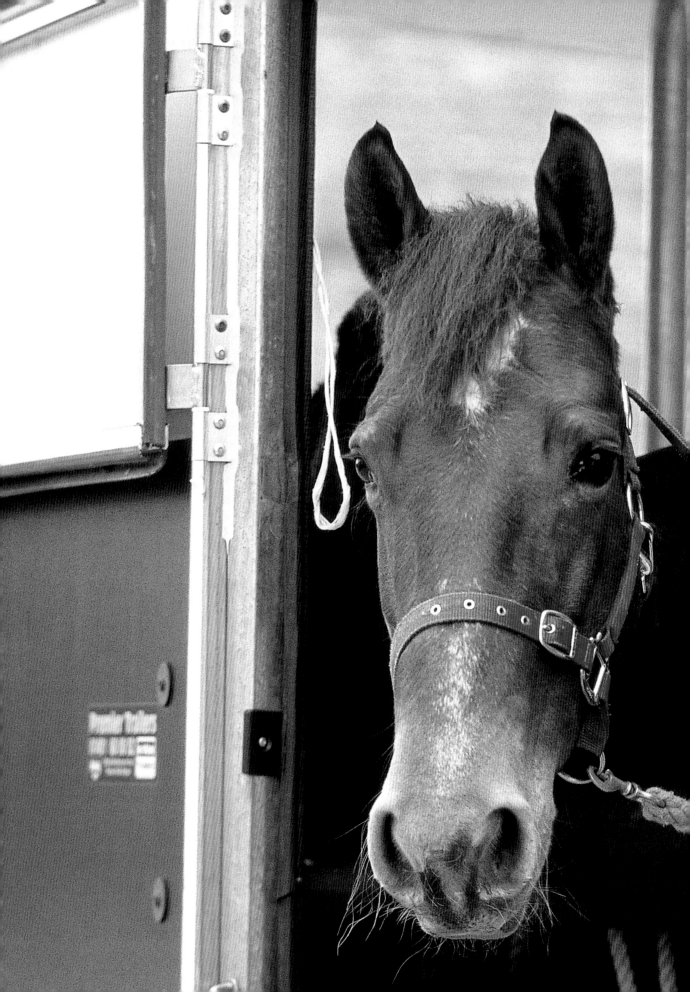

3 On False Ground

From our human perspective, it is surprisingly tough for a horse to step onto a suspicious-looking surface. Unfortunately for the horse this scenario is one of the most common that we ask him to face, whether we want him to walk through a puddle or up the ramp of a trailer or horse lorry. From the horse's point of view, jeopardising his ability to flee by risking his footing is a big deal, which is made more stressful by his naturally poor ability to judge distances directly in front of him due to his limited field of forward vision. All this aside, asking a horse to walk over a tarpaulin, or through a river crossing is well within his capability and he needs to learn to accomplish these tasks calmly and confidently.

Working over a tarpaulin

A tarpaulin is a good obstacle to use to get horses to start thinking rationally about problems and their solutions. Such safe but challenging work builds them up so they realize that they are more capable than they believe. Long lining over a tarpaulin is good training for any false ground work, such as soft going, water and so on, because it is teaching a horse to listen to direction from the bit.

At first, the horse will be wary of this strange obstacle in front of him and will need time to look at it and consider it. He may want to sniff at it. If he does take a tentative step onto it, he may then scare himself. The initial response of many horses will be to want to go around it and avoid it altogether. Their reaction to a request to walk over it is a good indicator of how much trust they have in us.

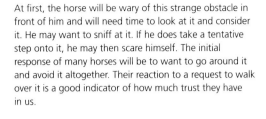

The principles are the same whether you lead or long line – ask the horse to consider your request and give him time; if he objects to considering, hassle him, but reward him by leaving him alone when he does make a positive move. If he wants to rush or jump the tarpaulin let him be free in his mouth, don't haul on him, but once he's done his jump over, then redirect him as soon as possible. Have the reins trailing so that you can slip them through your hand, but be careful not to get them caught on anything.

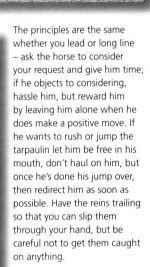

At the beginning

- Make it as easy as possible, but challenging enough that it develops the horse. For example, it is best to start with a tarpaulin that is folded in half or even smaller, and gradually open it up as you repeat the exercise.

- Before long lining over, lead the horse over because then you're at his head, which is what he is used to. Long lining is more difficult because you are behind him.

Once the horse is happy with being long lined over the tarpaulin, progress to riding over it. Here, a horse is asked to walk over a tarpaulin in the middle of an open field. There are no obstacles around, so he has the temptation to go to either side of it, but if the training has been thorough then he should think about what is wanted and try his best to do it for the rider.

Just as with the long reins, it is important to allow a horse a certain amount of freedom through his body in this situation so he doesn't feel restricted by you. Be ready for him to leap or move quickly over the canvas, but don't tense up. Direct left and right to get a forward movement – this is more effective than kicking – and the instant you get it, reward with a rub on the neck. Recognizing the smallest try and rewarding it is the key to the horse understanding what you want.

ask a harder question

When they are asked to walk on or over something that they don't recognize, horses will often want to test the ground by having a really good look. This is a self-preservation instinct and perfectly acceptable. This horse is showing how important it is to have the freedom in the reins be able to reach down over. Asking a horse to walk over a mattress is a harder question than the tarpaulin because the horse will be aware of a change of texture under his feet. This type of work is a useful precursor to introducing a horse to slightly soft or boggy ground.

The all-terrain horse

Look for ways to challenge your horse by finding different obstacles that have a different feel and make different sounds when he walks over them. Whatever the obstacle, it is important to remember that once a horse starts moving forward towards it, you should leave him alone and allow him to do it in the way he wants to. Stay in the middle and in balance. Don't interfere with your horse's balance, or try to help him find a route – a horse is perfectly capable of finding his own balance but this might mean he needs to put his head down or up as he goes. Give some leeway to left or right but keep the focus in the direction you want to go. Have fun with the variety of obstacles you try, as this develops the rational side of the horse's brain. It teaches horses to listen to and trust their riders, and it increases their confidence, which they really enjoy.

When they trust the person who is doing the asking, horses are capable of performing extraordinary feats. Climbing soft mounds of earth or stone, walking over soggy mattresses or going up and down steps – there is little that a horse can't do. And, once successfully completed, each of these challenges will increase a horse's self confidence as well as improve his relationship with his handler.

Going through water

With water you are once again going up in the level of the challenge. The horse doesn't know what depth the water is, so he has to trust you to know that you are asking him something that he is capable of doing. Water is a natural obstacle for horses, even if they are sceptical of it, but once they allow themselves the first few steps they will be happy to go. Carry out the same approach as you did for the tarpaulin: ask for one step and reward it as soon as the horse gives it. Eventually he will give you more. When I approach an obstacle that I know a horse will be wary of, I ask for forward movement by directing each side of him separately, rather than as a whole. This makes it easier to get a horse to move forward (see also pages 114–17). I like to think of it as riding the stride underneath me, rather than looking forward to a stride I haven't yet got.

This rider is not very committed to the task in hand and has not separated her right side from her left side, which means she is not getting positive forward movement **(1)**.

The horse whips around and she allows him to do so. It is so important to maintain direction, allow a little bit of lateral movement, but not enough that you allow him to get halfway home. Remember, you aren't a passenger **(2–3)**. Think about yourself as a guide to your horse and concentrate on helping him through his problem. If your horse does whip around don't grip on. Don't anticipate a problem either, as the horse will pick up on it, but be ready to diffuse a situation if necessary. The horse decides his final option is to plant himself and refuse to move forwards **(4)**.

4

I make the approach to the water **(1)**, clearly separating the two sides of the horse (see also pages 114–15). I allow him to have a good look at the obstacle while keeping the forward focus and intent. This gives him a chance to think about what I am asking and rationalize that it is not such a difficult task. He makes the decision to step into the water **(2)** and I go with him and let him know that it was the right choice **(3–4)**. He could even get to quite like water **(5–6)**!

3

6

repeat the process

Once a horse is comfortable with going through the water, repeat the process a few times so that he really understands that it is not a big thing. Jumping into water is a progression of this work.

trust is important

One day I had to ask my horse Tommy to go through a stream that had risen to about 1.2m (4ft) after heavy rain. It was a big request and I could almost hear him thinking, but he did it for me because of all the work we had done previously. Basically, he trusted me not to ask something that was impossible for him to do.

Jumping a ditch

Horses are often very intimidated by empty holes in the ground, such as ditches and hollows. If they are forced to approach a ditch against their better judgement, they will often shy away or rush and catleap over it. Again the trick is to let them know that there is nothing to be frightened of and to give them a chance to really think about what they are doing. They are going against their instincts in approaching calmly and not trying to run away – their instincts tell them that something could jump out at them – but it will give them a tremendous sense of relief to realize that there is no danger.

1

4

coping with napping

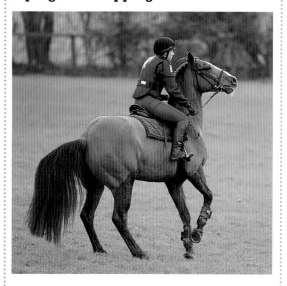

This horse is already napping even though he is still about 10m (30ft) away from this ditch jump. The rider carries out some damage limitation work, accepting that the horse is going to rear up and whip around at the sight of this jump. She attempts to redirect him, but because she has brought her hands down to prevent the rear, she has adversely affected her balance and control. Raising her hands would have allowed her to maintain her safe position (see also pages 114–15).

6

1 I work on the approach to the ditch by directing one stride and then another: just raising a hand up and out from the shoulder to get it moving is a good way of producing forward movement.

2 At the same time I make sure the horse keeps looking at the obstacle and give him plenty of rewards for each tiny try. The closer he gets to the ditch, the more difficult he finds this work.

3 I make sure that he knows that I won't bully him at this stage.

4 When he arrives at the ditch I give him the time and space to investigate. I wait until he makes the decision on the next move. If he whips around then I'll correct him but it is important not to hassle him here. I want to allow him to make his own choice.

5 He reaches towards the ditch by moving his back feet, so gets a reward. He wants to do as I ask but doesn't know that he can do it. To be hard on him at this stage means he will lose trust.

6 His decision to jump it comes in an instant, and I go with him. It's important to go with your horse with your reins loose if he jumps like this, so that he can move unhindered.

7–8 Once the foundations have been laid, we do consolidation work, approaching in walk again several times and then repeating the whole thing in trot.

Loading into a lorry or trailer

It is asking a lot of a horse to accept being enclosed in a small moving rattling space like a lorry or a trailer, and I tend to make this discipline one of the last things they learn during their basic training. Until you've got some kind of rapport with a horse and taught him the basics of leading and handling, you can't realistically expect him to come willingly with you into a vehicle. Obviously, there are times when a horse has to be loaded before you've had the opportunity to teach him all the basics, but the ideal is to get these things in place first. Even with the basic handling and leading in place, loading is still quite a daunting prospect for a horse but you'll have a better chance of getting a genuine decision from him

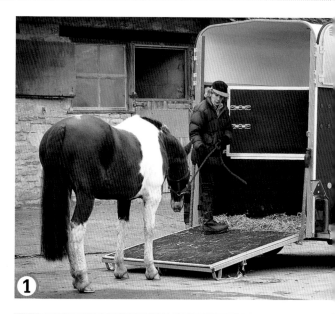

1 The owner is asking the horse to move forward, but she's not allowing him time to consider the question. He wants to sniff the ramp and ensure he is happy with what she's asking, but she's in a rush to get him on board.

2 She continues to try to load him by pulling directly forward. If she took a step to her left and asked the horse to move his right shoulder, it would free him up to move forwards, but she prefers to try to physically pull him onto the trailer (which, of course, she can't do).

3 You can see from the horse's quarters that all his thoughts, and therefore direction of movement, are backwards. Sadly, it is fairly clear that this horse doesn't want to co-operate with his owner. His body language says it all. There is a barrier between the two; its almost as if they don't like each other and the resentment has built up over the years.

light and stable

Horses can be wary of the dark interior of a trailer. Help your horse by opening the front ramp and taking out the partitions. Hitch the trailer to a vehicle so that it doesn't rock when the horse gets on it.

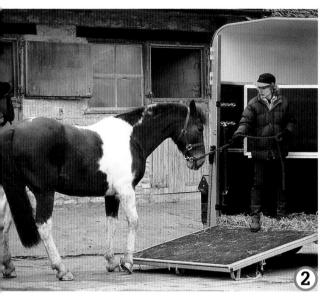

②

the principles of loading

- The principles of loading are the same as with crossing a tarpaulin or going over a ditch.

- Direct the horse's attention on the minutest level and then release and reward. If the horse only *thinks* about loading, then reward him.

- Be prepared to give him all the time he needs and don't rush him.

- You'll find his effort may swing between trying to load and trying to evade you. If his attention drifts, politely bring it back to where it should be.

- Your job is to keep him trying, so when he does make sure you reward him with a rub on the head. This will make him want to try harder for you.

- Keep everything calm and don't get in a fight with your horse.

- When he finally makes a decision to go for it and puts his foot on the ramp make sure you stay out of his way so as not to hinder any forward movement.

- Also, if he puts his foot on the ramp, don't feel you've got to hold him to it. Some horses take a step forwards, scare themselves and then step back and you should allow this, reassure and then encourage them to try the step again.

- If you try to hold a horse to a decision it can make him feel too restricted, which will lead to him pulling back and being reluctant to try again.

- It is important that you have an idea of what is going on in your horse's head. Notice when he is trying and when he isn't, and be prepared to be tougher when he isn't trying.

- Don't put on too much pressure, though, otherwise there's a risk he'll say, 'Right, I'm definitely not doing it.' On the other hand, if you're too easy, he'll say, 'Oh well, I won't bother.' Relate your rewards to the size of the try. A big try deserves a big reward.

plan your approach

- View loading as a training exercise to work on over a few days.
- Split the work into three parts: loading, closing the ramp, and travelling.
- Establish each part before moving on to the next – don't bring an inexperienced horse to the vehicle with the intention of loading and travelling all in the same session.
- Make the first few journeys short – don't load the horse, put him through a long journey, then expect him to be happy about getting on board next time.

When I take over, I use a quarter loop around the horse's quarters (see page 46). This is to help get the back feet moving if the horse won't move them at all and you get the situation where he is stretching from front to back. The loop cues the back feet into moving; it is not intended to drag the horse around.

Once he puts his front feet on a ramp I give him time to think about this and reward him. At this point, don't get excited and think your horse is nearly loaded, though. And, if he decides to back off the ramp, allow him to do so. He has tried and just needs a few seconds' break. If you allow this then he is likely to try again, if you don't then he is more likely to resist continuing loading.

Eventually, the horse walks on to the ramp and into the trailer without the encouragement of the quarter loop. This is enough work for the day and he will be rewarded by the lesson ending for now.

4 Out and About

It makes sense to do all your early work with your horse in the comfort of his own surroundings where you have control over the environment and can introduce him gradually to some of the many challenges he will eventually meet when he goes out and about into the big wide world. In this way, you can lay the foundations of the sort of responses and behaviour that you want from him, too. While, initially, you cannot expect your horse to feel as confident in a strange setting as he does in his own environment, it is vital to remember that your emotions will have an effect on him. If you can remain calm and centred, concentrating on getting the job done with as little fuss as possible, you will be a great asset to your horse. He will be greatly reassured by your behaviour. Horses are extremely sensitive and will always notice and react to their rider's emotions.

Accustoming your horse to sudden movement

Rope work is an extension of handling a horse. It teaches the horse that unknown and fast-moving objects can approach from either side and may look scary but aren't necessarily dangerous. This is good preparation for the type of general handling horses need to accept such as having a rug thrown over their back or a saddle pad put on, for example. When rope work is done well it helps them to learn that just because they don't know what something is, it doesn't mean it is going to harm them.

Stand quite close and gently flick the rope near the horse, starting in front of the withers. As he gets more comfortable and accepting, you can move behind his withers and further back along his body. Look forward to a point when you can throw a longer rope from further away without him feeling the need to move away.

I don't want the horse to move so I am standing just forward of his shoulder so that it is clear to him that I'm blocking his forward movement. He is calm and relaxed as we proceed. If I were facing the other way, he would know that I wanted him to move into the space I had made for him. My position, body language and the way I throw the rope, signal to the horse that I intend him to stand still. Work to increase his responsiveness to the handler (see pages 60–65) has taught him the basics of this, and this exercise is reinforcing that work and building on it.

exercise for the grey cells

This work is not intended to desensitize the horse, we are asking him to think about and then deal with what is happening. He needs to remain sensitive to what you are asking him of him. Make sure that you adjust the intensity with which you move the rope, so that he understands that you don't want him to move away from it.

The spookier, the better!

The more a horse sees, the more he is likely to be able to accept day-to-day things, such as children jumping on a trampoline. Here I have set up a few straightforward challenges for these horses to improve their self-confidence. Walking through a washing line laden with clothes is easy to practise at home and a useful test as this is the sort of thing that a horse might spook at when out riding.

1 Allow the horse to look at the line. Acknowledge when he is considering doing as you ask and reward him at that point with a rub on the neck or by allowing him to stand for a few seconds, but don't allow him to lose his attention. Getting this right is down to timing, which comes with practice.

2 When the horse responds correctly – going under the washing line – enable him to do this with freedom in his body and relaxed reins. Set up the situation and then allow him to make the move without restriction.

plan your approach

1 Introduce new objects in a safe, unpressured environment.

2 Be ready for a reaction, but don't tense up. Keep calm yourself by remembering to breathe.

3 Reward your horse for responding calmly, and never punish him for an instinctive reaction.

4 Allow your horse to see an unusual object from different angles – he won't always be completely comfortable until he has.

5 Studies have shown that horses need to repeat an experience, so ride your horse past a scary object a few times. He should become calmer each time.

With strange objects, such as tents, allow the horse to go wide initially and then she'll come to the point when curiosity makes her look closer – perhaps spooking a few times, first. Familiarizing a horse to things in this sort of situation helps them to become more trusting of what they've been asked to do. Eventually, a horse will walk past this type of obstacle without even looking.

1

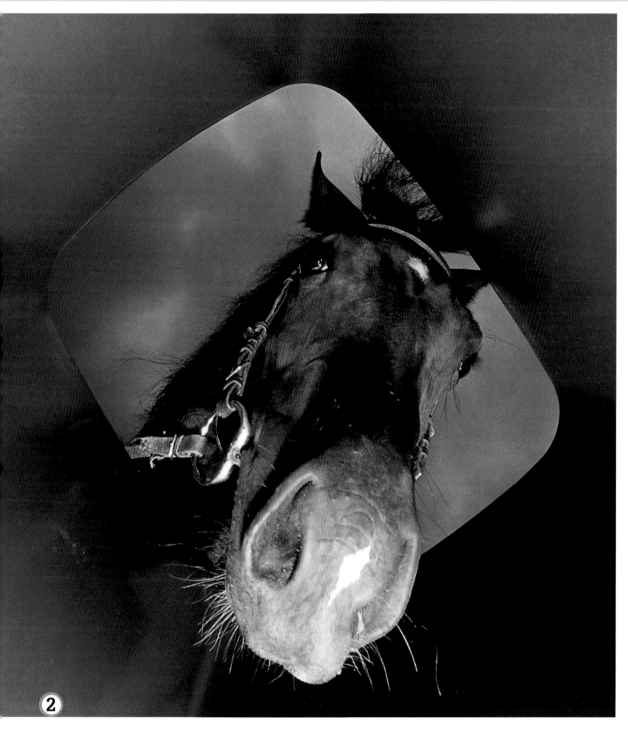

2

1 This horse has allowed herself to look into a wheelie bin. Horses are naturally sceptical of new things, but once they are encouraged to investigate, they will do so with interest, which enables them to learn that something is harmless. Some horses take longer to get to this point than others: simply give them more time and encouragement to help them take the correct option.

2 Anybody home? Once her interest has been aroused, the mare takes a good look into the bin, which just goes to show that with the right encouragement a horse will consider anything.

Meeting other animals

Meeting animals is increasing the challenge for your horse because animals move about and are unpredictable. To progress onto this stage, you have to be sure that your horse has faith in you and will respond to what you are asking of him. This type of work will provide your horse with invaluable confidence when out hacking. For example, if you meet dogs, you will be able to ask him to head them off, and take the heat out of the situation, rather than turn tail and run. At home with well-trained dogs you can gradually increase the intensity of the experience before going out.

1 Initially, I have my dogs lying down so the horse can approach them safely; with less predictable dogs ask someone to hold them on a lead or even tie them up. Don't attempt this work with a dog that is likely to bark or be aggressive towards the horse, or with one that might be afraid.

3 I've gone to head down the dogs with the horse sending them off. This work has given her more confidence. She feels she's in control and can manipulate the dogs.

2 Once the mare relaxes, the dogs are allowed to come closer. Keep your horse's attention looking forward but if he wants to move around a little that is fine. I let a horse move about 90 degrees each way but not further, otherwise they are considering flight. The key is to keep the horse considering the object that you want him to – that is where his focus is.

Keep him on the ball

- When allowing your horse time to consider an object, you need to maintain a certain level of intensity, otherwise he is quite capable of turning off and dozing on the spot.
- Don't stand too far away from the object or give him too much time.
- Be proactive but not aggressive. Make sure you are really asking him to consider the object.

make a cake

Training a horse is like baking a cake – is not just time, it's getting all the other ingredients right. So for example, this work doesn't rely only on your confidence as a rider, it's also a matter of distance from the dogs and the intensity of your intention.

Passing through narrow spaces

Generally, a horse will consider going through a narrow space the first time, but it's when they learn it could be a problem that they get upset – if they catch themselves or the rider's leg, for example. This work through narrow spaces shows them that if they do touch themselves on something on both sides it is not the end of the world. Start with a big gap and gradually reduce its size as the horse becomes more comfortable. The idea is for him to learn that it is his responsibility to walk through the middle rather than touch the sides.

1 As we approach this narrow gap, it is clear that the horse is thinking – I can't do this – and is searching for a way out with his right ear turned backwards.

I ask for a forward movement **(2)** and once he moves I direct him through the centre **(3)** without hindering him at all, but giving him a pat so he knows he's got it right. If a horse tends to rush, don't grab hold of him or try to slow him down as this increases the tension and pressure and makes him even more inclined to rush. Go with the rush. Allow it for the first few times and, so long as there's never any trauma associated with the gap, he'll work out that there is no need to speed and will slow down by himself.

make it easy

If you think you will be tense when your horse rushes through the gap, long rein him through to start with. Progress to riding through, when you are both confident.

1 Narrow barrels are more of a challenge, taking the level up one more stage. It is unlikely that a horse will ever have to do this or assert his authority to this degree, but it is still a useful experience for him. Again, it is also a confidence builder.

2 You can see the sense of achievement on this horse's face as he walks through the barrels. Even though they fall down around him, he barely shows any concern.

3 At first the horse thinks he can't do what is being asked and then he discovers he can. This is about building strength of character, which you help him to do. I feel that if you teach a horse about his strength then he won't use it against you.

① **②** **③**

Getting through gates

Every horse should be able to perform the necessary manoeuvres that enable you to open a gate from his back. It is such a basic skill and annoying and somewhat ridiculous to have to get off each time you come to a gate, on a hack or going into the arena. Learning how to open gates gives you an opportunity to school your horse as there are several schooling moves that you can do, such as backing and turning on the forehand, during opening a gate. Make sure that he knows each of these individually before putting them together like this. If your horse doesn't stand still to open a gate then go back to earlier in his training. Working on this technique will show how much a horse is listening to you, and will reveal whether you have got control of the front and back end and can move them independently.

1 Break down the manoeuvre, first opening and closing the gate from the horse, without going through it. Approach the gate, reach over to the latch.

2 Ask the horse to move over so you can open the gate, close the latch again and step back. Here, I've left space for her to move without banging herself on the post. Repeat this until the horse stands and moves aside without a problem.

3 When you eventually go through the gate, ask the horse for a turn on the forehand, which will swing her quarters around the gate so that you can shut it. This horse is particularly anxious, and giving her something positive to do is part of her schooling schedule. She doesn't have to do it perfectly.

remember

1 Gates shouldn't worry horses. It is quite logical for a horse to walk through a gate – they do it regularly when coming into the yard or going out to the paddock.
2 Make your aids clear and consistent.
3 Think about your position in relation to the gate.
4 Practise negotiating narrow gaps (p.110).

prepare and practise

Most of this work should be done without a gate at first. Take it slowly and be very clear with your instructions. If your horse still gets anxious: break down the actions into steps and practise them one at a time, perhaps in a school.

Overcoming napping

Napping can occur when you are trying to ride out on your own, or when leaving other horses during a ride. It is an irritating and sometimes nerve-racking habit that reveals gaps in a horse's training. Part of a horse's job is to be independent of other horses. For this reason, I like to get youngsters out and about on their own.

In fact, I rarely use a lead horse because I want to be sure the youngster is listening to me rather than purely watching what another horse is doing and, therefore, not taking any notice of me. It is fine to ride in company but it shouldn't be done at the expense of the horse's education.

safety first

I was once hacking with another rider and we came to a busy road that we needed to cross. The other rider saw a gap in the traffic and went for it. Being a second or two behind them, it was not, safe for me to follow. This is just the sort of situation where you must be able to rely on your horse coping with being separated from its pals. It could be a lifesaver.

These two horses work nicely together, but the piebald on the left has developed a dislike of going out on his own. He uses napping to make his feelings felt. Napping is an evasion through the shoulder and it needs a certain technique to overcome it once the horse has started.

When the horse begins to nap, the rider puts so much energy into kicking him forward that she forgets to direct him to where she wants to go, leaving him to push further in the direction that he wants to go anyway. She is also trying to use her left hand to push the horse back onto line, which is not effective. The key here is to direct the horse from the front end so his attention is where you want him to be. For example, here the horse is napping left. The rider needs to raise her right hand up and move it out to open a space for the horse's right shoulder to move into. She needs to have her weight in the right stirrup and use her left leg on the girth to push the shoulder over.

1 Here we have set up a natural situation where the horse might want to nap. Remember, you should be able to ask your horse to turn around and leave when you want him to. If he resists then he should be corrected.

2 When I ask him to turn away, his mind resists the idea and his attention is back on the other horse, but he does as I ask. Any evasion will always be in the shoulder. The shoulder therefore has to be correct – often people try to alter the quarters, but the quarters haven't done anything wrong.

3 I raise my hand to get that shoulder around and have my outside leg ready to bump the shoulder if necessary. You need to time the cues correctly so that as soon as the horse takes the right step he gets a reward and feels better.

4 He is still a little reluctant, but is prepared to continue. In this sort of situation it is fine to be sympathetic about your horse's dilemma, but remember he needs to respect what you are asking of him. He is not in the position to have an opinion.

looking pretty

Riders are often inhibited about altering their own riding position in order to give the horse the correct instructions. Be prepared to adapt to be effective. Do what is necessary at the time to get the result you need. You can then go back to the 'correct' position.

Better jumping

First attempt at fence

In the early stages of teaching a horse to jump always set up a fence that you know she can cope with easily. This is important for two reasons: it means that the horse can feel confident about what you are asking of her, and it means that if you sense she is going to refuse, you know that you can push her through it without feeling that you are asking too much. You need to be quite precise in your instructions. Don't give her the impression that you aren't sure of yourself as this will do nothing for her confidence.

1 You can see 'I don't like jumping' written on this horse's face. This is the point where you need to keep a horse's attention on the jump and back up your request with what ever you need. Come around the school to the fence with the attitude that you are going to jump it, but be ready to correct instantly if the horse says 'no'.

2 I don't let this mare's attention deviate from the jump at all. This is a reasonable jump for her to do. So when she doubts her ability to get over it, I can be sure I am asking a perfectly fair question. Here, I'm switching from raising one hand to raising the other, to bring her attention and shoulder back on line.

soft but strong

Be prepared to use seat, legs and hands aids when they are needed, but remain relaxed and loose until this time. This way you use as little and as much as is necessary to get the job done.

3 As the horse goes to duck right, I'm ready with my left rein to bring her attention back to the jump. I've got my weight in my left stirrup with my right leg on the girth to get that shoulder back on line. This all happens very quickly so you have to be prepared to react in a second.

4 She finds it in herself to consider the jump, but she's still not entirely convinced. This is fine, because this type of work is all about challenging horses in order to develop their character. Like any development programmes, sometimes it has to be uncomfortable in order to progress.

5 She's made a move with her back legs, which I praise but I can feel there is a tendency to shift her weight to the left, so I keep this rein raised while I acknowledge her attempt with a pat with my right hand.

6 Yes I can do this. When she makes her decision, she cat jumps and I go with the movement softly and loosely to stay with her. Whatever style of jump she does, it is important at this point not to pull back and to be close to her, so that she doesn't receive any conflicting signals from the rider.

Second attempt at fence

Repetition works wonders, as long as what you're repeating is good. You can see tension in the mare on the approach but sensing she will make an attempt without too much fuss, I get out of her way and let her go. Because she's tried left and right evasion already and neither was rewarding for her, she doesn't attempt to try them again. Although it might seem to go against the grain for many riders, a long rein gives more freedom to open your hands out and correct the shoulders if necessary, whereas if the horse ducks around to left or right, a short rein will pull you out of the saddle.

Third attempt at fence

After about three jumps over the fence, the mare now trots into it nicely. I allow her to reach down as she wishes and take off on a loose rein. It is important for her to work out for herself how best to get over the fence. This gives her a chance to think for herself and become neater and more assured. She is making a better shape and is picking her feet up tidily.

make it watertight

Always be totally committed to what you are asking your horse to do. Horses will exploit a loophole instantaneously, and will try harder next time if they gain even a second's benefit from an evasion.

improving an older horse

With a more experienced horse, I would go through the same procedure but I would be tougher and less sensitive, giving less room for manoeuvre. Allow the horse to find his own speed and if he wants to go on a stride, let him.

Getting ready for traffic

It is inevitable that at some point you will have to ride on the road, and when you do it is important that you have a horse that trusts you and will listen to you in all situations. This means that you need to have instilled a certain amount of knowledge in him about what he is likely to meet on the roads. True schooling in traffic can only be done on the roads but there is plenty that can be done in preparation. On the plus side, on most occasions, unlike dogs or livestock (see page 128), traffic is fairly predictable. Start your work in a safe environment and introduce your horse to any mechanical objects that are loud and clank.

Even if your horse is good in traffic, it is a good experience for both of you to see some of the more unusual mechanical objects that you might come across on your hacks. In a familiar environment your horse will feel safer, which will make him more inquisitive and prepared to investigate.

Don't forget that although you know what this is, your horse may never have seen one before, and he won't necessarily make the connection with the lawnmower or with a tractor, either, so take it slowly and gently and be prepared for his reaction.

We had the opportunity to introduce our horse to a dumper truck – stationary and then moving. At first I rode past it in the middle of the school, where there was plenty of space, then I asked a more challenging question by riding through the narrower gap at the side of the school (left).

Later on, I set up a meeting with the dumper truck while out on a hack (below). It is all good experience because, while few of us would welcome this type of encounter, sometimes it simply can't be avoided. Luckily, drivers of such vehicles are usually very considerate and will stop for you to go past and wait for you to ride on before moving off. The work done earlier (pages 110–11) has paid dividends here as this horse is accepting a fairly pressurized situation.

The tall hedge and narrow verges on this lane increase the sense of claustrophobia. Low hedges have the advantage of allowing a rider to see into the distance and get an early warning of oncoming vehicles, and wide verges provide safer passing places.

In order to do their job, police horses have to be 100% relaxed and happy with traffic. The horses that are used for police work are just ordinary animals and, as with any horse, their training has to begin somewhere. Usually, as here, work on traffic begins in a safe environment and progresses to real-life situations as the horses gain experience and confidence. The principles used for training police horses are the same as for when introducing any horse something new – I keep a loose rein and forward motion. I exploit the inquisitive nature of the horse, and give praise when it is deserved. After being introduced to a stationary Landrover, the horse is then asked to approach it when it has its headlights and blue flashing lights on. This increases the level of the pressure on a horse, and tests his training and confidence.

Police horse training is incremental with the pressure and challenges being increased and widened to ensure a well-rounded education. Once the horse is comfortable sniffing and looking at a vehicle, such as a tractor, the next goal is to be able to ride past it without him taking much notice.

ensure success

1 Relax – remember a horse will feed off your emotions, and if you get tense then so will he.
2 Set up an obstacle that you know the horse can cope with, even if at first he thinks he can't.
3 Work in a calm environment without too many distractions.
4 Avoid working on a day when you feel rushed or cross or when the weather is unpleasant.
5 Be prepared for something to take as long as it takes – don't ever rush.

When they are out on the streets police horses must be unflappable, no matter what happens around them. Street cleaners are just one of the vehicles they are likely to meet in their day-to-day work. It is easy to see how they could be disturbed by this type of activity behind them, so their training includes introductions to as many vehicles as possible.

Roadside obstacles

Police-horse training includes getting a horse familiar with objects that they'll encounter on the side of the road, such as road markings and salt bins. This is useful for all horses that will be ridden on the road and helps to teach them not to duck away from such items and into the traffic. Again this work is started in a safe environment, where the horse won't hurt himself or do anyone else any harm, and progresses to more realistic situations.

Although we know what a sand box is, remember that a horse's experience is gained only from what he sees from his paddock or stable, or when you take him out. Give him time to make up his mind and praise him for any attempts to investigate and accept new objects.

be roadwise

1 Be considerate to other road users.
2 Trot past parked vehicles and around corners so any vehicles behind you won't be held up for too long.
3 If an oncoming vehicle stops to wait for you to come past, trot where it is safe, again to reduce their waiting time.
4 Don't ride side-by-side when there is traffic behind you.
5 On narrow roads, pull in to enable vehicles to pass as soon as you see the opportunity.
6 Horse riders can appear arrogant and uncaring to other road users, so make sure you thank drivers who show you consideration.
7 Even in bright light, riders can be invisible to other road users. Always wear something reflective.

If possible choose a road with speed bumps on it as a first introduction to busy roads. The speed bumps ensure that traffic will already be going fairly slowly, which reduces the chance of your horse becoming uncomfortable or spooking as vehicles go past.

Introducing the horse to an unknown object (sequence above) nearly always follows the same procedure. Allow him to have a look and be ready for him to try to turn tail. Don't allow him to turn more than 90 degrees either way, otherwise you have lost control of his direction of movement. Once he has started to look at the object, he has started to accept it, but still be prepared for him to make the split-second decision to run away.

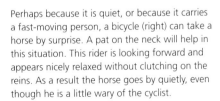

Perhaps because it is quiet, or because it carries a fast-moving person, a bicycle (right) can take a horse by surprise. A pat on the neck will help in this situation. This rider is looking forward and appears nicely relaxed without clutching on the reins. As a result the horse goes by quietly, even though he is a little wary of the cyclist.

Riding through smoke

Smoke is a spooky thing for horses, perhaps because it changes direction and they can't tell where it's going, or perhaps because of their innate fear of fire. This muck-heap fire offered me an opportunity to challenge this horse and build up his character. Although it is a reasonably rare challenge to encounter, the time when you are likely to come across smoke is on a windy autumn day, when someone has lit a bonfire to get rid of fallen leaves or some hedge prunings. As autumn can be a time when horses are a bit spooky anyway, it will be helpful if your horse is already familiar with smoke and accepts your instructions to walk past calmly.

This is the same horse that I worked through the barrels earlier (see page 111). You can see that he is thoughtful about this situation but that there is no real fear and he is working hard to fulfil my instructions. In all new situations this is the sort of behaviour you expect.

use a whipwhop

If your horse is inclined to stop and shut down, use a whipwop. Swing it in a big arc in front of you to hassle him into forward movement. Get your timing spot on – as soon as he moves, stop using the whipwhop, as soon as he stops, start moving it.

The horse is working forwards politely but also letting me know that he is wary. As I raise my hands, his ears cock towards them listening to what I have to say.

As we move beyond the smoke his trust in me increases and he accepts that what I am asking him to do is safe. This is a positive experience as he has come through safely and it makes him feel better about himself, too.

Meeting livestock

Most horses these days are raised in purely equine establishments where they don't come across livestock such as cows and sheep. As a result they can have some odd reactions when they first meet them. Some horses are absolutely terrified. It is important that you don't overface a horse in this situation.

Start by introducing your horse to sheep because they are more easily moved away, whereas cows are instantly curious about what has walked into the field and will come over to investigate. If the horse feels intimidated by this and tries to run away, the cows will chase it, which is exactly the wrong sort of introduction.

graduating to cows

- It is essential to have a person on the ground to head off the cows if they decide to rush over.

- Eventually the person can drop back, leaving the horse to do the work and move the cows around.

- When properly done, the horse will start to enjoy playing this game, changing the cows' direction and so on.

- Don't attempt this sort of work until you are sure your horse trusts you implicitly and that you have control over his movements.

Start with someone on the ground in front of the horse ready to move the sheep aside and allow the horse to step into the area, this gives him confidence in his ability to move the sheep. Keep everything calm – you don't want to upset the sheep. You can get the horse to move the sheep left and right like a sheepdog. Once he knows that the sheep will move away, he won't worry. Don't do this sort of work without permission from the sheep's owner.

Going to events

With a completely novice horse, introduce him to shows by going to small local events. Get the horse ready as if you are going to enter a class, but simply use this as an experience for the first couple of times and don't add the pressure of actually competing. Walking around a small show, watching other competitors and seeing lots of other horses can be more than enough for an inexperienced horse. Keep the pressure off him and do everything you can to make this a positive experience. Depending on his response, you can plan to enter next time. Keep going to small events until you are sure he can cope.

Your horse's first show will be an eye-opener for him! Help him to take in the bustle by being quiet and calm yourself.

plan your day

1 If you have to travel to a show, practise loading and transporting well before the day.
2 Familiarize your horse to being around more than one or two other horses by going to a small clinic. Clinics have the added advantage of having an instructor who will be able to give you confidence and who is on your side.
3 Introduce your horse to loud noises (the public address system) and bunting in a safe environment beforehand.
4 Get your tack and other equipment ready the day beforehand, so you don't raise the pressure by rushing around first thing.
5 Take a calm and experienced friend along, even if it is just to give you moral support and buy cups of tea.
6 Remember that shows are mostly just for fun, and so have fun.

5 The 100% Horse

On the whole, horses are very genuine creatures and want to please people. With a little patience and a sympathetic, progressive training programme, it is amazing how much you can train them to do. Activities that seem completely alien to them, such as walking up and down steps, over strange surfaces or under flapping objects, can become everyday occurrences that they don't bat an eyelid at. However, in order to achieve this level of trust in a horse, you need to be consistent, fair and thorough in your training. Horses that have specific jobs to do, such as police or army horses, receive greater levels of training than most, and therefore seem to be extremely impressive. The good news is that any horse can learn to be unflappable – the power to achieve this lies in the hands of the trainer.

Let's play ball

Working with a ball is a good way to get horse and rider to relax. In a way, you are almost humouring the horse who begins to think that people are rather odd. Here the ball is under our control and this is a fun exercise for this police horse, but this sort of experience could come in handy in helping your horse stay calm if you came across a ball game while on a hack. Basically, though, this type of work is just another exercise aimed at asking a horse to stop and think about what he is seeing without immediately dismissing it or panicking.

2 We show him that it is not fixed to the ground, and this intrigues him. Although you can see that he is slightly wary here, he gradually realizes that it is not so odd and that it is not going to hurt him. This work develops a horse's left-brain ability by focusing on getting him to stop and think about things rather than do what he's evolved to do, which is to turn around and run away.

1 When the horse sees the ball for the first time you can see that he is bowled over by it, but there is more fascination than worry on his face.

3 Soon he is almost ignoring our ball game. This is obviously thanks to all the work that has been leading up to this moment, but horses can be remarkably accepting of almost any activity going on around them, so long as they are not being hurt by it.

4 Throwing the ball over his head is a way to increase the pressure on the horse and ensure that he has seen and accepted the ball, rather than just ignored it.

5 The horse becomes quite relaxed with the ball appearing from all directions. I keep his attention on the ball so he has no reason to be surprised or to panic.

reinforcing the lesson

1 To make sure that the horse has really accepted the ball, we try some ball playing inside, which is also another step on the ladder of experience.

2 Altering the surroundings means there are different distractions for the horse, which might make him slightly more reactive.

3 The ball bounces back, which changes the experience, too.

4 We do this work on another day, so that we don't overface the horse and he has time to think about what he has already learned.

5 We also give the horse plenty of breaks during this sort of training, and, as always, plenty of rewards for doing the right thing.

Football crazy!

Once they have finished their training, police horses go on to work in real-life situations, such as football crowd control where there might be people throwing things. To ensure they can cope with the additional tension, we take the pressure up a level by moving the ball around much more quickly and loosely. The horse is a little worried by this but works through it. It is important not to overface him at any stage, so the person on the ground needs to be sympathetic. I keep the horse looking at the object, this will keep his mind on it and compel him to think about it. He begins to take it all in his stride and we finish on a good note.

The more thoroughly a police horse is trained, the less stress he will experience during his day-to-day work. It isn't only about accepting a ball coming at him in all directions, it is also about him learning to trust his rider and listen to him, no matter what else is going on around him. Many horses prefer someone else to take some of the responsibility for decisions, but they need to be sure that they can trust the decision-maker.

concentrate on the front end

When a horse whips his front end around it is more difficult to stay on than if he moves his back end. If he tries to move his forehand, keep his head around to stop this as much as possible.

Walking over objects

Police horses are trained systematically to walk over odd things on the ground so that they go unquestioningly, say over drain covers and across soft ground on fields, and will listen to their rider in any situation. They know that if they're asked to do something, it's safe; their rider won't ask them to walk onto something that might injure them. This type of work can be a huge leap of faith for a horse so it is important, once again, to give plenty of rewards and be sympathetic and encouraging, while allowing him to do it his way by giving him freedom through the reins and going with him when he makes the decision.

1 This is a continuation of false ground work (pages 83–99) with more pressure from the reflective police riot shields and other objects placed around the school. The horse hones in on what he is being asked to do. It is down to the rider to focus him, so that although he will be aware of what is around him, he knows he doesn't have to worry about it.

2 He makes the decision to go, and leaps over the mattress. This is a typical over-reaction at this stage, but the horse needs to be able to try out various ways of dealing with the problem for himself. He has shown himself to be willing to consider what is being asked of him.

3 The pair comes around the school where there is another obstacle to negotiate. The horse is looking very warily at the mattress while the rider is being encouraging with his legs. Raising his arms alternately to loosen up the horse's shoulders would be a good way to get some more forward movement.

4 Again, when he makes the decision to go, it is rather rushed and the horse avoids stepping on the mattress. This can be hard work for a horse: all their instincts tell them to avoid ground that they know is soft because it could be dangerous.

praise when praise is due

It is vital to get the timing right when you reward. For example, the instant the horse makes a step onto the mattress, give him a pat or release the leg pressure. If you wait until he is hesitating again, you are rewarding the wrong behaviour.

testing your horse

- Have some fun by setting up an obstacle course. Get some friends to join in.
- Introduce the horse to each obstacle separately and then gradually put them together.
- If you find any of the obstacles seem to be a particular problem for your horse, refer to the relevant part of this book for help.

Horses avoid stepping on people at all costs and it is a measure of this horse's trust that he steps onto this dummy. Of course, he will not be required to walk on people in his work, but he might need to pass close to large objects on the ground that he doesn't recognize. This work simply continues to instil in him the need to listen to and trust his rider implicitly.

5 Gradually, this horse accepts that he is not being asked to do anything impossible, or dangerous, and brings himself to walk onto the mattress. This will be rewarded with lavish praise and then we will repeat the exercise until it is well established in his mind.

Umbrellas

Once horses have overcome their fear of one thing, they are more willing to try considering others. Umbrellas are considered spooky by many horses. Think of it from the horse's point of view: here is a large often brightly coloured thing moving around on human legs!

The speed with which umbrellas appear, opening up suddenly, can also be a problem. It is possible to help a horse through his concerns, which will make hacks on rainy days far less stressful. Police horses, as here, need to learn about umbrellas to be able to do their job.

Open the umbrella in a secure (not windy) area and bring the horse in and work him around it, gradually bringing him up close to the umbrella. The important thing is to start work at a distance from the umbrella that your horse is comfortable with and slowly decrease the distance so that his tolerance is increased.

As the horse starts to relax you can pick up the umbrella and start to increase the exposure, going up through the pressure levels. Have a long lead rope so that there is space for the horse to move away.

The horse is slightly concerned at this view of the umbrella, but although he puts his head up, he decides not to move away.

The aim is to get to a position where you are carrying the umbrella like a pedestrian would and can approach the horse with it without him becoming scared. Here he is fairly relaxed and is more inquisitive about the umbrella than worried by it.

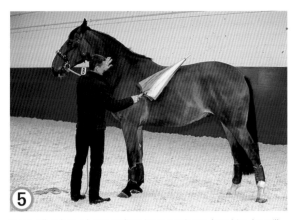

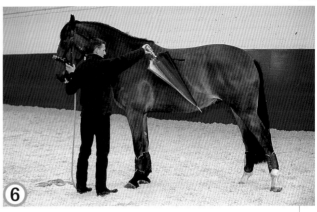

5 Eventually when a horse realizes it's not going to hurt him, he will allow you to touch him with the umbrella and even have it open over him.

6 If you decide to do this, make sure you work methodically over his whole body, both sides, so that you ensure he really accepts what is happening.

7 This sort of procedure is really a repetition of that used for introducing a horse to many objects that he might otherwise be rather wary about, including numnahs, rugs and plastic bags.

8 When I open the umbrella over him, he decides to make a sideways step, but on the whole he is relaxed and unconcerned – look at the expression on his face and his general demeanour.

If you want to take it to the ultimate stage you could ride him with it but it isn't necessary. This photograph is included to show how much a horse will learn to accept, so long as the training is thorough and thoughtful.

Flapping objects

Horses tend to be wary of flapping objects, such as flags, laundry on a washing line, birds flying up in front of them or plastic bags caught on branches, particularly on a windy day, when a horse is a little more reactive than usual anyway. Police horses learn about flapping objects as part of their overall training, and it would make your rides more enjoyable, and safer, if you could rely on your horse not to shy or spin round if he came across a similar scary object. Again, this type of work is another step on the way to having the unflappable horse, a horse you can rely on to do as you ask, no matter what the situation (see also pages 102–105).

1 This horse has planted himself and is not going to move forwards until he has decided what to do, but the decision is difficult for him to make. It would be wrong for the rider to try to kick him into movement without getting his mind back to him, because the horse could go anywhere. The first thing is get his attention.

2 Although he is making some movement, the horse is really trying to ignore the flag and side step around it, in the hopes that this will satisfy his rider. However, he has at least made a decision, and is going with it, so he is learning.

3 When I get on I think forwards and ask the horse to move towards where I am thinking. I maintain the positive thought that what I ask and the way I ask it will work. In this situation, think through the obstacle to the other side.

4 As we approach the obstacle, I stay low and behind the horse's head. Make sure you don't interfere with the obstacle. Remember to stay effective and keep looking forward – get him moving on a line before you start bending down to get under the obstacle.

5 You can see my positive thought has carried this horse through. He is a little sceptical, but he has no intention of refusing to do as I ask. He walks positively forward with a workman-like attitude.

Negotiating steps

This work is focused on developing responsibility. Basically, we've introduced an obstacle and it is up to the horse to accept his part of the deal, which is to walk forward positively and confront it. Our responsibility is not to hinder him, to stay balanced and allow him freedom. Going up and down steps isn't something many horses have to do but is a possibility for police horses. The work shows the level of trust you can achieve and the level of responsibility that a horse will take, once he understands what he is being asked.

horses have brains

It is tempting for us to think our horse won't know where to put his feet on steps. In fact, a horse can see very well and knows what he is doing with each of his feet. He may jump because this is easiest, not because he doesn't know how to place his feet on each step.

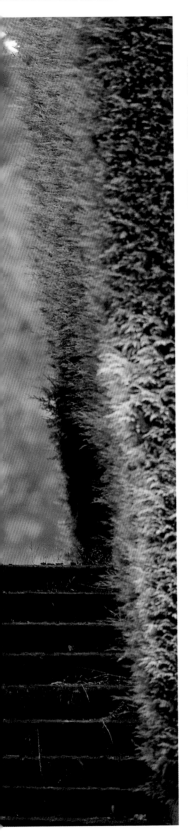

For a horse, going up steps is like going up a short, steep slope and he will probably want to do it as quickly as possible. You can see the effort in his quarters as he leaps up on his first attempt. However, gradually he realizes that it could be easier and very soon he is walking up and down (see overleaf) as if he has been doing it all his life.

The horse is a bit surprised by this sudden drop in front of him, but makes the decision to do as his rider asks. As he comes down the steps, it is the rider's job to make sure that the horse puts his feet in the right place and stays balanced. The temptation for the horse is to jump, because it is easier for him than thinking carefully about where he needs to put each foot on the way down. At first the rider will allow him to do this if that is what he decides, but eventually, through repetition, he will learn to walk quietly down.

what use is this to my horse?

While you might not want to take your horse's training this far, encouraging him to take responsibility for his actions and to make the right choices for himself is key to training him to meet a wide variety of challenges. Do not be restricted by what convention says a horse can or can't do – as you can see in this section of the book, horses are capable of much more than we might imagine.

Pulling it all together

By now you will have realized that horses are capable of much more than many of us ever expect of them. The limit to your horse's training lies in your own mind. If you are willing to invest in the thought and planning, and spend the time necessary, you can train your horse to accept and do a wide variety of activities and all in all be a real pleasure to have around. This in turn will make your own life much easier and less stressful – and, of course, you will be giving your horse the best possible chance of a successful life, especially if the unthinkable happens and you have to sell him. He or she is much more likely to find a good home if he is easy to look after and 'do' in all respects: in other words is 100%.

In order to improve your horse and your relationship with him, you first need to see life from his point of view. There is no point trying to train him using methods that he does not understand. For example, look back through this book – you won't find a single place where the horse is drawn into a confrontational situation, because this is not the best way to train a horse. When horses are forced or bullied into something, they don't understand what they have done, or why they have done it and they can build up a sense of resentment towards the skill or the person enforcing it. Most of the work towards having a 100% horse is done at a level well below confrontation, building the horse's confidence and allowing him to work towards making his own decision and finding a solution that will benefit him, not just for this moment but for the whole of his life from now on.

The training also takes place once any possible sources of pain or resentment are removed. It is vital that horse owners understand and act upon the fact that a horse's behaviour is rooted in a cause: *horses do not stand in their stables dreaming up ways to annoy their riders, just for the hell of it*. Their behaviour is often a direct way of communicating an issue they have, such as pain or discomfort – so take time to listen.

Creating a 100% horse takes time and effort – on your part as well as your horse's – but the rewards are superb. While the end result is impressive, many people who follow this approach soon realize that the journey itself is well worthwhile. Along the way to educating your horse for life, you will reap numerous benefits yourself: learning a new way to approach problems, building a great relationship with your horse, realizing that you can control your own emotions, learning a lot about yourself and so on... Go on give it a go, as someone said 'You have nothing to lose and everything to gain.'

Adopt an 'almost anything' approach towards training your horse, and you'll find a change in his attitude too. Give him every chance and he'll impress you!

always watch for ouch or ow

Imagine if someone made you run a half marathon in training shoes that were a size too small. You'd be in pain and feeling very resentful. A horse can feel just the same if forced to perform wearing a saddle that pinches him every time he moves, or made to jump even though he is suffering pain in his joints. Horses have feelings and deserve to be treated with respect.

Twelve tips for success

1 Set everything up for success – control the factors that are within your power, such as your horse's physical and mental comfort, the time available for working with your horse, your own emotions.

2 Have a clear idea of what you are trying to achieve for each session, but be flexible about your goals so that you can work with the horse how he is at that particular moment.

3 Deal with the horse as he is on the day – don't expect him to be as good as yesterday, don't punish him if he is not, just work with what he can offer today.

4 Ensure your training plan is logical and progressive.

5 Work with respect and attention to detail.

6 Do not make assumptions about your horse or yourself.

7 Be aware of how your horse is viewing the situation.

8 Work with the horse in a practical way. You both have responsibilities if your partnership is to work and it is important that both parties accept and act upon their individual roles.

9 Reward your horse for the slightest try – and hassle him if he is not trying. Hassle doesn't mean punish, it means insist that he does pay attention and does address the problem facing him. Punishing a horse when he is trying to deal with a problem doesn't achieve anything.

10 Make learning enjoyable for your horse, and for yourself! While repetition is important for learning and for consolidating information and skills, it can have a negative effect if done to excess. Consider your horse's personality – some horses are very quick on the uptake and will soon start to use their brains against you if they are bored.

11 If you hit problems, go back a step and consolidate the basics before trying to move on again.

12 Keep a diary. It's often difficult to recognize how much progress you are both making on a daily basis.

...and look for the penny to drop

Sometimes it takes very little for a horse to understand what you want and to start to do it, and often, once he's done it once he will continue to do it each time he's asked. Watch your horse, if he's got it, don't keep on making him do it just for practice. Think about something you've learnt to do, such as reversing a car. Once you know how to do it properly and well, imagine how annoying would it be if someone kept asking you to do it, again and again...

Useful Information

Michael Peace and Think Equus

Michael offers private consultations, group clinics and lecture demonstrations. As well as accepting horses for schooling at his yard in Oxfordshire, he will work with you and your horse at home. The ideas and processes behind Think Equus can also be applied to business training.

Contact Michael at
PO Box 230,
Kidlington,
Oxfordshire
OX5 2TU.
Tel/fax: 01865 842806.
e-mail: michael@thinkequus.com

Equine Muscle Release Therapy (EMRT)

Adapted from the Bowen technique, EMRT was developed by Alison Goward in Australia. It works on the muscle and soft tissue fascia at specific neuro-muscular trigger points on the body. It activates the horse's healing mechanisms to release muscle spasms and address skeletal imbalances, and to increase blood supply to the affected areas. It also increases lymphatic drainage, so that dysfunction debris, which interferes with healthy muscle and joint activity, is cleared away.

Lesley Bayley is an Equine Muscle Release Therapy practitioner.
Tel: 07774 226204.

McTimoney Chiropractic

To find out more about chiropractic and find a practitioner in your area, contact:

McTimoney Chiropractic Association
3 Oxford Court
St James Road
Brackley
Northants NN13 7XY
Tel: +44 (0) 1280 705050
www.mctimoney-chiropractic.org

In the US, www.chiroweb.com is a good starting point.

Note: *Before any therapist treats your horse you must, by law, gain your vet's consent. Most vets are very happy to give this and may be able to suggest suitable complementary practitioners.*

Books and other media

Clipping (DVD) Michael Peace.
  Many of the basic skills your horse needs to know are covered in this DVD as they are all needed in order to overcome clipping problems.
The Q & A Guide to Understanding Your Horse Michael Peace and Lesley Bayley (David & Charles).
The Photographic Guide to Schooling Your Horse Lesley Bayley (David & Charles).
Think Like Your Horse Michael Peace and Lesley Bayley (David & Charles).
A video of the same name is also available.
The Visible Horse by Susan Harris and Peggy Brown (video, Trafalgar Square Publishing)
  This is a good introduction to the horse's skeleton and muscles.

Index